WHAT YOUR COLLEAGUES ARE SAYING . . .

Leading With Intention *delves into a complex topic, but makes it a "tight" read. Every chapter has charts, focused checklists, and reflective tools. Systemness is always helped by "interaction" effects of core factors. This book will help you focus and integrate through self-awareness and self-efficacy, connection and inquiry, and intentional professional learning that generates impact.*

—Michael Fullan, Professor Emeritus, OISE/University of Toronto, Ontario, Canada

Leading With Intention *provides valuable insights that encourage "leaning in rather than leaning away" from our collective responsibility for student learning. DeWitt and Nelson have crafted a powerful guide inviting readers to harness thoughtful and genuine relationships to cultivate a legacy of learning.*

—Kimberly M. Fry, Assistant Executive Director, Professional Learning, Former School Principal and District Superintendent, Washington Association of School Administrators, Olympia, WA

Education is in a tough spot. The only sustainable way out is through intentional leadership and connection. Peter M. DeWitt and Michael Nelson provide the roadmap here in Leading With Intention.

—Danny Bauer, Ruckus Maker & Do School Different™ Designer, Better Leaders better Schools, Bestselling Author, Syracuse, NY

Leading With Intention *is an excellent resource for educational leaders aiming to deepen their impact on student learning and build stronger connections within their school community. Through a skillful blend of practical insights, research, and personal stories, authors Peter M. DeWitt and Michael Nelson articulate a vision for leadership that underscores the importance of self-awareness and human interconnectedness, providing a foundation for effective decision-making.*

—Valerie Page Truesdale, Senior Assistant Executive Director, The School Superintendents Association Alexandria, VA

For Britt, who always knew.

For Doug.

Leading With Intention

Leading With Intention

How School Leaders Can Unlock Deeper Collaboration and Drive Results

Peter M. DeWitt

Michael Nelson

Foreword by John Hattie
Afterword by Shelley Harwayne

For information:

Corwin
A Sage Company
2455 Teller Road
Thousand Oaks, California 91320
(800) 233-9936
www.corwin.com

Sage Publications Ltd.
1 Oliver's Yard
55 City Road
London EC1Y 1SP
United Kingdom

Sage Publications India Pvt. Ltd.
Unit No 323-333, Third Floor, F-Block
International Trade Tower Nehru Place
New Delhi 110 019
India

Sage Publications Asia-Pacific Pte. Ltd.
18 Cross Street #10-10/11/12
China Square Central
Singapore 048423

Vice President and Editorial Director:
    Monica Eckman
Senior Acquisitions Editor: Tanya Ghans
Content Development Manager:
    Desirée A. Bartlett
Senior Editorial Assistant: Nyle De Leon
Production Editor: Vijayakumar
Copy Editor: Melinda Masson
Typesetter: TNQ Tech Pvt. Ltd.
Proofreader: Girish Sharma
Indexer: TNQ Tech Pvt. Ltd.
Cover Designer: Gail Buschman
Marketing Manager: Melissa Duclos

Printed in the United States of America

Library of Congress Cataloging-in-Publication Data

Names: DeWitt, Peter M., author. | Nelson, Michael, author.

Title: Leading with intention : how school leaders can unlock deeper collaboration and drive results / Peter M. DeWitt, Michael Nelson.

Description: Thousand Oaks, California : Corwin Press, [2024] | Includes bibliographical references and index.

Identifiers: LCCN 2024012466 | ISBN 9781071924419 (paperback) | ISBN 9781071947876 (adobe pdf) | ISBN 9781071947890 (epub) | ISBN 9781071947883 (epub)

Subjects: LCSH: Educational leadership. | School management and organization. | Professional learning communities.

Classification: LCC LB2806 .D486 2024 | DDC 371.2–dc23/eng/20240415

LC record available at https://lccn.loc.gov/2024012466

This book is printed on acid-free paper.

24 25 26 27 28 10 9 8 7 6 5 4 3 2 1

Contents

Foreword

One of my passions lies in translating the messages of Visible Learning into the realm of sports coaching. We have successfully applied these principles to elite rugby, cricket, soccer, Australian rules football, baseball, and ice hockey. Coaching is a form of teaching, so it is no surprise that there is a great deal of overlap between the classroom and the sports field. Coaches, akin to teachers, can provide an amazing amount of feedback and often pride themselves on how well training sessions go. But in the game, things often turn to custard.

Sport is based on a simple premise – exploiting opponents' errors and weaknesses. Elite players have a remarkably high level of game-savvy; they can efficiently exploit weaknesses and devise strategies on the fly. They capitalize on instant feedback during the game with the aim of hearing, understanding, and putting feedback into action. They know how to play the game alone and as part of the team, and they understand that lapses in attention or mistakes can be exploited by the opposing side.

Much of the feedback that coaches offer during a game goes unheard and, more importantly, is often given too late to provide any meaningful impact. The feedback is mostly about the game, the strategies, and the next moves. It is rarely about the thinking in the player's heads as they play the game. Great coaches train for chaos, for mistakes, for optimizing opportunities, and for team bonding. Great coaches might advise a team player who makes a mistake that has important negative effects on the team, that it is ok to be upset for five seconds but then they must forget it. Great coaches help players to both acknowledge their emotions and also not let those emotions hinder future actions.

Timothy Gallwey, in his impressive book *The Inner Game of Tennis* (2015) argues that in competitive sports, we play not against one, but two opponents. The "outer" opponent is the other players/team, but we also play against an "inner opponent" – our own mind that can create obstacles like self-doubt, disappointment about letting down the team, low self-efficacy, concentration lapses, and nervousness. Gallwey noted tennis players talking to themselves with comments like "try harder", "why do I not know this?" and asked, "Who is talking to whom?" His answer was that we are speaking to two selves: Self 1 is the conscious mind, which is often judgmental and critical, and Self 2 is our body, nervous system, and unconscious mind. Self 2 physically performs and plays the game, but it is only when Self 1 and 2 are aligned that we get peak performance.

Gallwey's coaching focused on bringing Self 1 and Self 2 into alignment: that is, bringing together the performance and the person. He identified four steps: (1) have the student/player observe without judgement; (2) make them think or relive the observations with images, feelings, and imagination; (3) have a go and try the thinking ("Just do it"); and (4) observe what they practices without judgement.

This philosophy can be extended to the inner game of leaders. Leaders, like elite sports players, are constantly observed and these observers intuit the leader's motivations and beliefs. The message in *Leading With Intention* is that the leaders need to anticipate, know, and reflect on how others see and interpret them. Leaders need to spend more time seeing the impact of their performance and person – and preferably bringing these together into "one" person. Leaders have to be superb listeners – of their Self 1 and 2. They need to be internally and externally self-aware, hear what others are saying and thinking, and demonstrate to others that they have understood what has been said (although they do not have to agree). An example is trust – trust is what you are when you walk into a room, it is your being and credibility in the eyes of others, it is based on the actions you have made from prior encounters, it is a function of your skills at active listening, and it is the bringing together of your performance and person.

The core notions discussed in DeWitt and Nelson's book are the essence of being aware of Self 1 and Self 2 and include self-awareness, fostering human interconnectedness, engaging in collective inquiry, promoting professional learning and development, showing confidence and self-efficacy, and designing your own learning environment. The last element is core to schools – why should we make it compulsory for students to attend school and then not insist all adults in the schools also attend professional learning? You and your staff need to be continually growing, learning, and passionately working to improve your impact.

Every decision you make is up for queries about alignment with what you say you are with how others see you. The task is to lead others to do and think in ways that improve the impact we all have on our students, and this requires high levels of people management, high levels of trust, and great skills at convincing others that it is in their and everyone's best interest to enact that which you as leader ask them to do.

No one said being a leader was easy. It requires high levels of confidence, extensive experience with communicating what you are asking others to do, a relentless focus on improvement, and most of all it entails listening to oneself as well as to others, communicating your beliefs, passions and ideas, and bringing others along with you on a worthwhile set of actions, all deeply constructed within a climate and culture worth defending. This book on unlocking deeper collaboration has the potential to drive meaningful results in leadership, highlighting the importance of self-awareness, transparent values, and effective communication in creating a culture worth defending.

—John Hattie

Acknowledgments

From Mike: This is my first book. As a result, I think about the many people during my nearly 40 years as an educator who saw things in me that I didn't see in myself. This includes Jan Donaldson (in memory), Sandra McCord, Tom VanderArk, Dale Holland, Mary Holland, Nancy Merrill, and Art Jarvis. Throughout this same time, I have worked with hundreds of colleagues who have supported me in becoming a better educator and have become lifelong friends, for which I am grateful. I am appreciative of Helene Parroff, Pat Large, Gerrie Garton (in memory), and Jill Burnes.

It was at the launch of the Instructional Leadership Network almost three years ago that I began working with Peter in supporting the incredible teaching and learning leaders across the state of Washington. We encouraged and nudged each other as colleagues and quickly became friends. I am deeply honored that he would consider me as a co-author for a book. We are both grateful that the impact of the network continues to have a rippling effect in Washington.

I'm a self-admitted emotional person particularly when it comes to thinking about my own children. I stand in awe of our son, Hans, and daughter, Anna. They are kind, loving, and generous humans. I am tearing up as I write this. They have selected perfect partners in Amy and Brian and have gifted us with three grandchildren: Carter, Grant, and Maisie. Blessed doesn't even begin to describe the feeling I have when I think of them.

My biggest fan and champion as a person and a professional is my wife, Britt. She predicted this moment many times. I would laugh, but secretly I was hoping she would be right.

From Peter: I am grateful that Mike agreed to co-author this book with me. I could not have worked with a better co-author, colleague, and friend. As you read this book, you will learn from his stories and expertise, just as I did every time I had the opportunity to work with him. To me, this book is not just a co-authoring experience but a journey through our friendship and conversations.

Additionally, I am so grateful for the support of my family and friends. They have always provided me with strength and support and helped give me the confidence to do anything I wanted. We should always surround ourselves with people who support us and make us better, and my family and friends have certainly done that.

From both: We would like to thank Chris Beals, Tom Murphy, Jenni Donohoo, Kim Fry, Joel Aune, John Hattie, and Shelley Harwayne. Additionally, we spent time visiting schools talking with leaders and teachers about their practices while conceptualizing this book. Thank you to the leaders and teachers in the Woodland School District and Fife School District, which are both in the state of Washington.

PUBLISHER'S ACKNOWLEDGMENTS

Corwin gratefully acknowledges the contributions of the following reviewers:

Sean Beggin, Associate Principal
Anoka-Hennepin Secondary Technical Education Program
Andover, Minnesota

Jayne Ellspermann, Founder and CEO
Jayne Ellspermann, LLC, School Leadership Development
Ocala, Florida

Ronda J. Gray, Clinical Associate Professor
Decatur, Illinois

Kathy Rhodes, Principal
Hinton Elementary
Hinton, Iowa

Joy Rose, Retired High School Principal
Worthington, Ohio

About the Authors

Peter DeWitt (EdD) is the founder and CEO of the Instructional Leadership Collective. He was a K–5 teacher for 11 years and a principal for 8 years. For the last 10 years, he has been facilitating professional learning nationally and internationally based on the content of many of his best-selling educational books.

Peter's professional learning relationships are a monthly hybrid approach that includes both coaching and the facilitating of workshops on instructional leadership and collective efficacy. Additionally, in the summer of 2021, Peter created a yearlong on-demand, asynchronous coaching course through Thinkific where he has created a community of learners that includes K–12 educators in leadership positions.

Peter's work has been adopted at the state and university level, and he works with numerous school districts, school boards, regional networks, and ministries of education around North America, Australia, Europe, Asia, the Middle East, and the United Kingdom.

Peter writes the Finding Common Ground column for *Education Week*, which has been in circulation since 2011. In 2020, he co-created *Education Week*'s A Seat at the Table where he moderates conversations with experts around race, gender, sexual orientation, research, trauma, and many other educational topics.

He is the series editor for the Connected Educators Series (Corwin) and the Impact Series (Corwin) that include books by Viviane Robinson, Andy Hargreaves, Pasi Sahlberg, Yong Zhao, and Michael Fullan.

Peter is the 2013 School Administrators Association of New York State's (SAANYS) Outstanding Educator of the Year and the 2015 Education Blogger of the Year (Academy of Education Arts and Sciences), and he sits on numerous advisory boards.

"There is no more noble profession than that of an educator." That was what **Michael Nelson**'s mom said almost every day of his childhood. For almost 40 years, Mike has been an educator. His mom would be pleased.

Even though Mike still considers "teacher" as his primary title, he has served as principal, district instructional leader, and superintendent, and currently serves as assistant executive director developing programs and initiatives for superintendents and district leaders in the state of Washington.

Mike's leadership is based on the foundation value that is it necessary to develop a kind, compassionate, and empathetic culture rooted in belonging and equity. He describes his leadership work as building human connectedness, recognizing you must always model what you lead as you build teams of individuals supporting students in their learning. The Muckleshoot Indian Tribe awarded him with their official blanket for building a collaborative partnership between the Tribe and school district, the highest honor of the Tribe and the first time a non-Tribal member was selected to receive this blanket.

He has received many state and national awards during his time as a principal and superintendent. As a principal, he was acknowledged by Pacific Lutheran University as its Outstanding Recent Alumni in 1997. At the same time, the school he was leading as principal received the National Blue Ribbon Award from the U.S. Department of Education. As a superintendent, he was named Washington state's 2019 Superintendent of the Year. During his tenure as superintendent, Mike was elected president of the Washington Association of School Administrators (WASA) by his peers.

While WASA president, he was one of two superintendents in the nation selected to participate in the Embark Program facilitated by the U.S. Navy. He spent time on the USS *Ronald Reagan* learning from all levels of the men and women serving on this aircraft carrier. He also has received the Washington State Association of Supervision and Curriculum Development Educating the Whole Child Award.

Glossary of Terms

In schools, we often have a common language but not a common understanding around that language. When we look at educational leadership through an international lens, we know that we often don't even have a common language when it comes to the words used in schools.

To create a common language and common understanding, we here define the terms used in this book. This will help us as we work through international and cultural contexts.

Building leader: This is an administrative position where the leader must perform management duties as well as practice instructional leadership. Building leadership positions include school principals in the United States, Canada, and Australia and head teachers in the United Kingdom.

Collective leader efficacy: Collective leader efficacy is a school or district leadership team's ability to develop a shared understanding and engage in joint work that includes evaluating the impact they have on the learning of adults and students in a school.

District instructional committee: At the district level, there is often a district leadership team that may include the director of teaching and learning or assistant superintendent of curriculum and instruction, along with other district and building leaders, depending on the makeup of the district.

Faculty/staff meeting: A school gathering that may take place once or twice a month, where teachers and leaders learn together about ideas or innovations that impact students in positive ways.

Human interconnectedness: Human interconnectedness happens when individuals unite to build a stronger learning culture by authentically communicating with each other and challenging each other's thinking to create deeper and more intentional contributions.

Instructional leadership team: Instructional leadership teams are school-based or district-based teams. At the school building level, an instructional leadership team includes a principal, assistant principals, teacher leaders, and school staff such as school psychologists.

Joint work: Judith Warren Little (1990) defines joint work as "encounters among educators that rest on shared responsibility for the work of teaching (interdependence), collective conceptions of autonomy, support for teachers' initiative and leadership with regard to professional practice, and group affiliations grounded in professional work" (p. 519).

Knowledge: "The fact or condition of knowing something with familiarity gained through experience or association" (Merriam-Webster, n.d.).

Metacognition: How individuals think about their own thinking.

Professional learning and development: In *Call to Action: Bringing the Profession Back In,*

Michael Fullan and Andy Hargreaves (2016) write, "*Professional learning* is often like student learning—something that is deliberately structured and increasingly accepted because it can (to some) more obviously be linked to measurable outcomes... *Professional development* involves many aspects of learning but may also involve developing mindfulness, team building and team development, intellectual stimulation for its own sake, and reading good literature that prompts reflection on the human condition" (p. 3).

School building: This is a smaller system housed within a larger system such as a school district. In the United States, school leaders are sometimes referred to as school building leaders. School buildings, for all practical purposes, include grade levels or departments.

School district: A system that usually includes elementary, middle, junior high, and high schools. In countries like Canada, we may refer to these systems as divisions or school boards.

Skill: The ability to perform a task using previously acquired knowledge.

Teacher leaders: Teachers within a part-time or full-time leadership position where, in most cases, they do not have to evaluate their peers. Some teacher leadership positions are professional learning community (PLC) leads, department chairs, or middle-level leaders (Australia).

Understanding: An assimilation of an idea into what is already known.

Introduction: Putting It in Perspective

In this book, we invite you to be intentional about the legacy you will leave behind. The connectedness you build now with your colleagues and your network of learners will be long remembered by your staff. When we as professionals take the time to consider our legacy, our daily decisions alter slightly; they become deeper—a bit more intentional.

How do leaders develop stronger connections with their staff, students, and larger school community? Leaders don't always have the time to sit and ponder the countless decisions they are daily responsible for or to ponder whether those decisions build stronger connections or higher walls between them and the rest of their school community. What concerns us is that there are leaders who make decisions based on emotions over evidence. *Leading With Intention: How School Leaders Can Unlock Deeper Collaboration and Drive Results* is focused on helping leaders and teachers understand their thinking as educators, develop human interconnectedness as a school community, and engage in a reciprocal transfer of learning. This is a practical book, filled with research, content, stories, and places to process information, and it's focused on how we think, the choices we make when it comes to initiatives, and how we develop deeper academic and social-emotional connections with those with whom we work.

Leaders and teachers need time to process what they do, how they do it, and whom they do it with in order to move forward in positive ways to influence adult and student learning. This book will provide the space to process the information for those educators who want to put in the time.

Leaders and teachers need to understand who they are as learners. In *Leading With Intention*, we ask two fundamental questions:

- How do we, as leaders and teachers, engage in actions that have a positive impact on students?
- How do we, as teachers and leaders, evaluate our own impact?

Our experience has taught us that the most effective way to approach these questions is through stories. Research shows that stories can have a powerful impact on how we learn and how we engage with the learning. Your stories matter. Take the time to write your stories in this book when prompted because writing your own stories will help you understand your legacy as a leader and teacher.

Readers will be asked to engage in a metacognitive activity at the beginning of each chapter so that they are better prepared to tie their own learning needs to what is presented in the book. We begin each chapter with a KWLH chart, where we ask you to list what you know already about the topic, what you would like to learn, as well as what you have learned and how you feel you learned it. We ask that you consider the first two sections (KW) before reading each chapter and reserve the last two sections (LH) for filling out after you read it.

Throughout each chapter, there will be opportunities for reflection (*What's Your Story?*) and practical tips (*Leading With Intention*). You will also find stories about our experiences. This book will help leaders, teacher leaders, building leaders, and district leaders go from merely being on task to being deeply engaged in the work needed to not just impact student learning but also reconnect with why they entered the education profession in the first place.

This book focuses on the following areas:

- **Chapter 1: Self-Awareness.** We will focus on how self-awareness will make you not just a better leader but also a better learner. In meditation practices, there is often a focus called "being a witness" to our behaviors, reactions, and actions. Self-awareness is not just how we view ourselves, but how others view us.

- **Chapter 2: Fostering Human Interconnectedness.** Whether you are a school building leader, teacher leader, district leader, or facilitator of learning in workshops, it is important to foster a connectedness within the group around a common mission. Strong connections lead to deeper learning and impact.

- **Chapter 3: Collective Inquiry.** Due to a variety of situations that include being reactive, initiative fatigue, and a never-ending list of to-dos, we have found that leaders can lose sight of their true priorities for their school or district. We will help you define your three main priorities so that you can focus on them.

- **Chapter 4: Creating a Learning Network to Focus This Work.** Most facilitators of learning know why they are in a conference room facilitating learning, but we have found that many participants do not necessarily know why they are in the room. We will clearly define how leaders can take their priorities and connect them to the learning they attend.

- **Chapter 5: Creating Your Own Learning Environment.** Lastly, if you have developed self-awareness as a leader, learned ways to foster human interconnectedness, defined your priorities as a leader, and then learned the necessary elements of professional learning, you will be ready to design your own professional learning regardless of whether that learning is in a conference room, faculty meeting, or instructional leadership team meeting.

Our goal is that after reading this book, readers will

- Understand the importance of leadership self-awareness and metacognition
- Hone their human interconnectedness skills to help educators work in collectives
- Develop pedagogical knowledge to help focus initiatives on student learning
- Be able to set the conditions to engage in joint work
- Develop ideas about bringing a more coherent systemic focus to their work

We appreciate that you are willing to take this journey with us.

Mike and Peter

CHAPTER 1

Self-Awareness

> **By the end of this chapter, you will**
>
> - Engage with a metacognitive strategy that will help activate prior knowledge
>
> - Process the elements of leadership self-awareness and consider two or three actions you can take today
>
> - Be able to name two categories of self-awareness and relate them to your own self-awareness
>
> - Identify four archetypes of self-awareness and how they are related to context
>
> - Identify how leadership self-efficacy impacts what we do as leaders

Take some time to consider what you know about the topic of leadership self-awareness. Use the following KWLH chart to engage in that thinking. Write down some notes in the first two sections: "What do I *know*?" and "What do I *want to learn*?" Then turn that thinking into success criteria in the "By the end of this chapter" section.

At the end of the chapter, you can fill out the last two columns.

SELF-AWARENESS KWLH CHART

K	W	L	H
WHAT DO I KNOW?	WHAT DO I *WANT TO LEARN?*	WHAT HAVE I *LEARNED?*	*HOW DID I* LEARN IT?

By the end of this chapter, I want to...

-
-

WHAT IS YOUR SELF-AWARENESS ARCHETYPE?

There are multiple ways to look at and understand self-awareness. It's not as simple as knowing yourself because we may have blind spots when it comes to how we lead or interact with others. James Clear (2018) says, "We're so used to doing what we've always done that we don't stop to question whether it's the right thing to do at all. Many of our failures in performance are largely attributed to a lack of self-awareness" (p. 64). Fei Wang (2021) writes, "Self-awareness is a critical trait for school leaders and a significant predictor of the level of intrapersonal intelligence" (p. 406). And Elizabeth Perry (2022) suggests, "Self-awareness has two categories: internal and external self-awareness."

Internal self-awareness is crucial because it is the foundation for personal growth and self-improvement. When you deeply understand your thoughts, emotions, values, and behaviors, you are better equipped to make informed decisions, set

Intrapersonal intelligence

Self awareness

what we have always done, is it right, best?

meaningful goals, and manage your feelings effectively. This self-awareness allows you to align your actions and values. Additionally, it helps you as a leader identify your strengths and weaknesses, which will help you grow personally and professionally. Without internal self-awareness, you are at risk of struggling with self-doubt, inner conflict, and a lack of direction.

External self-awareness is equally as important because it relates to how others perceive you as a leader and how you interact with the community around you. Understanding how your actions and words impact others is vital to building strong relationships, developing effective communication, and engaging in impactful collaboration. External self-awareness enables you to adapt to diverse group dynamics and work effectively in collectives. Without external self-awareness, you are at risk of unintentionally alienating others, experiencing communication breakdowns, and missing opportunities for personal and professional growth. Perry (2022) adds, "We might think we don't need to worry about internal self-awareness if we have external self-awareness or vice versa. But balance is key. They require different strategies and skills to understand. We should aim to balance our vision of ourselves with how others see us." A combination of internal and external self-awareness is vital for achieving a well-rounded and emotionally intelligent approach to life and interpersonal relationships.

We believe there are four different ways to look at self-awareness through the lens of internal and external self-awareness. These four ways are organized in Figure 1.1.

FIGURE 1.1 • Self-Awareness Through the Lens of Internal and External Self-Awareness

	HIGH EXTERNAL SELF-AWARENESS	LOW EXTERNAL SELF-AWARENESS
High Internal Self-Awareness	Individuals deeply understand their thoughts, emotions, values, and behaviors. They are also highly attuned to how others perceive them, and able to accurately gauge the impact of their actions and words on those around them. These individuals are effective communicators, empathetic, and skilled at building solid relationships. They are often seen as emotionally intelligent	Individuals have a strong understanding of their own thoughts, emotions, values, and behaviors (high internal self-awareness). However, they may need to be more attuned to how others perceive them, or struggle to accurately gauge the impact of their actions on those around them (low external self-awareness). These individuals may be very self-reflective and clearly

(Continued)

Figure 1.1 (Continued)

	HIGH EXTERNAL SELF-AWARENESS	LOW EXTERNAL SELF-AWARENESS
	and capable of quickly navigating complex social situations.	understand their own identity and values. Still, they could find navigating social dynamics and adapting to various social contexts challenging.
Low Internal Self-Awareness	Individuals have limited insight into their thoughts, emotions, and behaviors (low internal self-awareness). However, they are highly perceptive of how others perceive them and are skilled at reading social cues and adjusting their behavior accordingly (high external self-awareness). While they may excel in social situations, they may struggle with understanding their motivations and emotions, potentially leading to inner conflict or a lack of authenticity in their interactions.	In this quadrant, individuals have limited insight into their own thoughts, emotions, values, and behaviors (low internal self-awareness). They may also need help understanding how others perceive them. They may need to be more skilled at reading social cues or adapting their behavior in different situations (low external self-awareness). These individuals may face challenges in personal growth, building strong relationships, and effectively communicating with others.

Source: DeWitt and Nelson (2024).

It's important to note that self-awareness can be developed and improved with practice and self-reflection. Each quadrant represents a different starting point, but individuals can enhance internal and external self-awareness to become more well rounded and effective personally and professionally.

This is a good time to pause and ask you to engage in the first set of Leading With Intention action steps. The action steps in this chapter focus on ways you might deepen your understanding of your own leadership self-awareness.

LEADING WITH INTENTION

If we don't know who we are as leaders, how can we understand which of our actions are successful or not successful? Looking at the four self-awareness archetypes in Figure 1.1, ask yourself, "How do I know for sure what category I am in?" To explore the answer to that question.

- **Send an anonymous leadership survey out to staff.** Only do this if you are prepared for how they might respond. Use the information to take meaningful action.

- **Take video.** During a district meeting, several one-on-one conversations, a professional learning session, or a faculty/staff meeting, videotape yourself. Prior to recording, explicitly identify what you want to learn.
- **Conduct empathy interviews.** Randomly select a group of individuals who you believe will tell you the truth, and have one-on-one conversations asking them to describe your level of leadership self-awareness. Know that these interviews take a great deal of trust.

Self-awareness is positively associated with job-related well-being, a greater appreciation of diversity, improved communication with colleagues, and increased confidence (Sutton et al., 2015), and we believe that the three suggested activities in the Leading With Intention section will provide some good avenues to improve your self-awareness.

LEADER, LEARNER, LISTENER

Practicing intentional leadership means having deeper relationships and focusing on developing interconnectedness. Use those relationships and connectedness to ask challenging questions, not because you want to cause conflict, but because you want to learn more. Additionally, intentional leadership means pursuing the expertise to have more impact on district, building, and classroom practices. Aim to see yourself as both the teacher and a learner.

Taking on the role of learner means that you need to find a balance between your confidence to lead in a situation and your openness to hear dissenting opinions. This is not easily done. Albert Bandura (2010) suggests, "Individuals who are highly assured in their capabilities and the effectiveness of their strategies are disinclined to seek discordant information that would suggest the need for corrective adjustments" (p. 183). Self-awareness also means understanding your level of confidence but being open to listening to dissenting opinions.

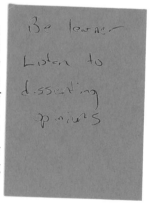

Be learner

Listen to dissenting opinions

We would like to pause right here and give you a moment to reflect on your leadership. In the introduction, we said that we want you to think about your legacy as a leader. Because this is hard to do during day-to-day activities, take the time to stop and do so now. This book is meant to be both one part learning from us, and one part learning from yourself.

WHAT'S YOUR STORY?

Who am I as a leader?

How do I find a balance between management and instructional leadership (a focus on learning)?

As a building leader or teacher leader, what do I due to understand whether our focus as a school transfers to the classroom?

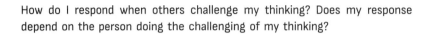

WHAT'S YOUR STORY?

How do I respond when others challenge my thinking? Does my response depend on the person doing the challenging of my thinking?

As a district leader, what do I due to understand whether our focus as a district transfers to each school within the district?

What are my success criteria as a leader? What do I believe a successful and impactful leader looks like, acts like, or sounds like?

We would like to offer one more space for you to practice self-awareness. James Clear (2018) affirms, "One of our greatest challenges in changing habits is maintaining awareness of what we are actually doing" (p. 64). He suggests we keep a list of our daily habits, and then write a + if it's a positive habit, a − if it's a negative habit, and an = if we see it as a neutral habit.

We believe that there is power to Clear's suggestion. An example might look like this:

MY DAILY HABITS AS A LEADER	
Entered the office	+
Turned on the coffee	=
Checked email	− (negative because it wasn't an emergency or crucial to do so)
Looked at social media focused on educators I follow	−
Walked around the building to say hello to teachers before the students entered	+
Stood in the foyer to welcome students	+
Had a meeting with admin team	+

Write a list of your daily habits as a leader, and indicate with a +, −, or = whether the habit is good, bad, or neutral. Self-awareness is about truly understanding ourselves and our actions. Being intentional about examining those actions is crucial to leadership.

MY DAILY HABITS AS A LEADER	POSITIVE + NEGATIVE − NEUTRAL =

Greet folks at duty +
Check in with MT +
Email −
Greet students +
Walk building

Only when you understand yourself as a leader can you engage with people on a deeper level, which requires seeking feedback. Bandura (2010) goes on to say that "the challenge is to preserve the considerable functional value of resilient self-efficacy, but to institute information monitoring and social feedback systems that help to identify practices that are beyond the point of utility" (p. 183). This is the heart of self-awareness.

Matthew Eriksen (2009) says that

> Self-awareness is having conscious knowledge about one's self, about one's beliefs, assumptions, organizing principles, and structure of feelings and their consequences on one's day-to-day lived experiences. (pp. 748–749)

Self-awareness is vital to engaging in deep and intentional leadership. In the following excerpt from a blog post Mike wrote in June 2023 called "How Superintendents Can Engage Board Members to Benefit Their Districts," you will see how Mike showed the self-awareness as a leader that his job was to get transitioning board members actively engaged in the professional learning of teachers and leaders so that the priorities of the district were not just clear to everyone but supported by the board and community as well.

Knowledge Through Storytelling

How Superintendents Can Engage Board Members to Benefit Their Districts

How can we get school board members to become advocates for the professional learning teachers need to have a deeper impact on student learning?

Too often, board members are seen as being disconnected from the day-to-day learning needs of teachers and students. They are seen as the people who focus on how the district spends money or how to keep a district from raising taxes. Although those are important aspects of the job, so is a focus on student learning—and the necessary learning teachers need to be more impactful in the classroom.

During my nearly 14 years as the superintendent in one district, a five-person board supervised me. And during those 14 years, 15 different people filled those five seats. Even though tenure of board members is generally longer than that of superintendents, it often feels like there is constant change. Gene Sharratt, a former superintendent in Washington state, shares, "If one member of a board and superintendent team is new, then you have a new team. Even though the change is one person, you must acknowledge and respond as if it is a new team."

In my case, I was the anomaly and the constant member of the team, serving about a decade longer than the average superintendent tenure (which recently retired AASA—The School Superintendents Association executive director Dan Domenech says hovers in the five-year range). Some may say it must have been difficult having so many different individuals supervise me. But from my perspective, all those transitions helped me stay focused on leading the board to home in on student and adult learning because I was always working with a *new team*.

In the state of Washington, the board sets local school district policy based on state law and supervises the superintendent. That's its purpose, as I heard so many times during my tenure. But if a superintendent only focuses on that function, they are not leveraging the influence that a united team of superintendent and board members could have in propelling the learning for both students and staff. This is where the influence of the "superintendent teacher" comes into play.

What Is a Superintendent Teacher?

A board and superintendent can move the focus on student and adult learning forward through their response to the necessary professional learning experiences that engage their staff members. However, the board should have a clear focus on what professional learning

experiences staff members need to do that work, and the board needs to take part in some of that learning to truly understand the needs of their teachers.

This is where the superintendent can take on the role of teacher for their board. The superintendent can provide the professional learning to the board that they need to help support teachers and students. Nancy Merrill, one of the longtime school board members with whom I worked, noted the experience of working collaboratively and the difference it made for them in terms of understanding the needs of students and staff—and, more generally, for the "power" of professional development.

For superintendents, here are five strategies for guiding board members to be advocates of professional learning in their districts:

- *Questioning*
- *Being present*
- *Listening to dialog*
- *Being a researcher*
- *Honoring*

Questioning

Most board members do not have a background in education. I have found that most want to support school district professional learning initiatives, but because of their background, they often remain quiet during staff presentations. That leaves staff members often wondering how the board truly feels about their work, and as a result, they make up their own narrative. *Wait, What?* by James E. Ryan (2017) is a book that I used to encourage board members to ask questions. Its premise focuses on five key question stems:

(Continued)

(Continued)

1. Wait, what?
2. I wonder...?
3. Couldn't we at least...?
4. How can I help?
5. What truly matters?

The first time we used this book, we read it as a team of six studying each question. After that, it was the first book given to new board members. We created a poster of the five questions that was placed near the board table so members could see them during presentations and help keep the board focused on student learning.

Being Present

From a superintendent's perspective, there is nothing more exciting than having board members who want to study and learn about best educational practices. In our system, our board members were invited to professional learning events. More frequently than not, a board member or two would join. This accomplished several things. First, our staff appreciated learning side by side with them. Second, the board members at the event would frequently report about it during their public meeting, which eventually made its way to all staff members and the district website.

Listening to Dialog

All elected officials need to be good listeners. I found it critically important to build background knowledge for my board about professional learning occurring in our system. When asked about professional learning in schools or out in the community, having background knowledge allowed board members to build a greater understanding of our district's work. Whether it was with a student,

a staff member, or a community member, the board's ability to engage in conversations about the work built an important level of credibility that spread throughout our system and community.

Being a Researcher

I never expected board members to read complete research articles or books. I would, however, offer both. Whenever we did a whole-staff book study, our board received a copy of the book. As superintendent, I felt it was my job to highlight snippets of importance for the board at board meetings and in my weekly Friday updates. During our board workshops or retreats, I could go deeper into the content of the book or article, processing the research using similar protocols that a principal might use with staff members.

When you create a team of six who want to be learners and support professional learning in the district, board members become learners themselves and will send you books, articles, and links to research they found. I embraced that. Many times, it was very good information with complementary insights to the professional learning going on in the system. I would share how this connected to our work. Even when the research didn't specifically match, fantastic dialog occurred to help us better solidify the vision of our professional learning purpose.

Honoring

Boards across our nation honor the professional learning going on in their districts. This is necessary as staff want to hear they are engaged in good work. The community also wants to hear that early release time for professional learning and money being spent on professional learning are valuable.

There is a difference in how the message is received. If the message is being given by a board that is not engaged in professional learning, staff and community know this. If, however, staff and community know the board's active role in professional learning, it is received in a more positive way.

The words may be exactly the same but felt and responded to differently. A staff member is more likely to feel honored when they are acknowledged by a board that is actively engaged in the professional learning process, too. The words are genuine, and the response is positively felt, rippling from staff and into the community.

The five concepts of *questioning, being present, listening to dialog, being a researcher,* and *honoring* are simple, yet led by a "superintendent teacher," a board can profoundly impact a school district in becoming one that supports and empowers professional learning.

Source: Adapted from Nelson (2023).

Mike's story highlights the importance of having leadership self-awareness. Many superintendents do not look at new school board members as an opportunity to learn about their own leadership, nor are they self-aware enough to inspire school board members to engage in the same professional learning teachers and leaders are engaged in to help develop a deeper understanding among their main priorities as a district.

WHAT'S YOUR STORY?

In Mike's story, he used the phrases *questioning*, *being present*, *listening to dialog*, *being a researcher*, and *honoring*. Write down your own story here describing a time when you engaged in those actions for others, whether as a teacher leader, a building leader, or a district leader.

FIVE SELF-AWARENESS QUESTIONS TO CONSIDER

Self-awareness gives you the ability to foster collaborative relationships that engage in joint work to identify a challenge or an innovation and take it from the surface level to a deep level of transfer within a classroom, school, or district. Peter Drucker (2005) writes,

> To do those things well, you'll need to cultivate a deep understanding of yourself—not only what your strengths and weaknesses are but also how you learn, how you work with others, what your values are, and where you can make the greatest contribution. (p. 2)

To do this work of self-awareness, Drucker says you need to answer five important questions.

1. *What are your strengths?*
   Drucker suggests that people are more likely to know what they are *not* good at than what they *are* good at. He recommends we write down our actions that are tied to our priorities and reflect 9 or 12 months later to see our actual results.

2. *How do you perform?*
   Drucker (2005) believes you need to spend time focusing on how you perform in your position:

   Amazingly few people know how they get things done. Indeed, most of us do not even know that different people work and perform differently. Too many people work in ways that are not their ways, and that almost guarantees nonperformance. (p. 4)

Part of what you need for practicing intentional leadership is an understanding of how you best take in information. Some of you do this through reading. You read research, long emails (you don't scan them!), and reviews about programs you wish to implement. Others of you do it through listening. You have listening tours where you engage in conversations with stakeholders, or you have committees where you use protocols to help you engage in in-depth conversations with those around the table. The importance is to know which one you are best at.

Drucker (2005) asks,

> The first thing to know is whether you are a reader or a listener. Far too few people even know that there are readers and listeners and that people are rarely both. Even fewer know which of the two they themselves are. (p. 4)

3. *What are your values?*
   What are your values, and do they line up with the values of your organization? Drucker (2005) says that if your values do not align with the values of your organization, then you will "not only be frustrated but also will not produce results" (p. 6).

4. *Where do you belong?*
   "A small number of people know very early where they belong. Mathematicians, musicians, and cooks, for instance, are usually mathematicians, musicians, and cooks by the time they are four or five years old" (Drucker, 2005, p. 7). For those of you in education, it may come down to understanding what position within a school works best for you (e.g., moving from teacher to principal or from principal to director) and knowing what position does not work for you.

5. *What can you contribute?*
   How do our strengths and values help us connect with ways to contribute to the greater good?
   Drucker's work around self-awareness, along with what we are laying out here in this chapter, means being aware of your strengths and blind spots. The only way to engage in that behavior is to surround yourself with diverse-minded people and set the conditions necessary to invite them to provide you with their perspectives even if those perspectives are different from your own.

WHAT'S YOUR STORY?

Take some time to reflect and write answers to Peter Drucker's (2005) questions.

What Are My Strengths?

How Do I Perform?

What Are My Values?

WHAT'S YOUR STORY?

Take some time to reflect and write answers to Peter Drucker's (2005) questions.

Where Do I Belong?

What Can I Contribute?

DO I NEED TO JUMP IN OR OBSERVE?

Let's take these questions from Drucker (2005) and go a little deeper. As a new school principal, I (Peter) was hired without any leadership experience. I had been teaching in a high-poverty city school district and was hired to take on a principalship in a rural area about 15 miles from my home. I engaged in a lot of proactive work before I officially started this position, like spending two days at the school, going over one late afternoon a week after my students went home for the day, or attending some board of education meetings in what would be my new school district. Those are examples of jumping right in because I was eager to learn and also develop relationships before I officially started the role.

However, I also knew when to wait and see where I fit in. I did not go in and try to make changes right away, because I knew that I first needed to understand where I fit into the school. Too often new principals want teachers to fit in around them, whereas the opposite is true. New leaders need to understand where they fit in, and take time to reflect on their own leadership practices and what they can learn from the situations taking place around them.

This takes self-awareness. Leaders who lack this level of awareness are more at risk to make hasty decisions that may lead to initiative fatigue because they may try to plug a hole in a problem without a true understanding of the root. This is where we see reactive (as opposed to proactive) leadership play out. We want leaders who take time to process and engage others before they define an adaptive challenge and try to solve it. To do this, leaders have to consider their own level of self-efficacy.

WHAT'S YOUR STORY?

Do you jump, or do you sit back to see where you fit in? Take some time to think of a situation where you jumped right in. Then think of another situation where you waited to see where you fit in.

I Jumped Right in When. . .

I Waited to See Where I Fit in When. . .

LEADERSHIP SELF-EFFICACY

Knowing when to jump in and when to see where we fit in takes self-efficacy. A common understanding of self-efficacy comes from Albert Bandura (1997):

> Self-efficacy refers to beliefs in one's capabilities to organize and execute the courses of action required to produce given attainments. . . . Such beliefs influence the courses of action people choose to pursue, how much effort they put forth in given endeavors, how long they will persevere in the face of obstacles and failures, their resilience to adversity, whether their thought patterns are self-hindering or self-aiding, how much stress or depression they experience in coping with taxing environmental demands, and the level of accomplishments they realize. (p. 3)

It's important for all of us to understand self-efficacy because people who seem resistant to ideas or initiatives may just lack the self-efficacy to do the work, but they don't feel comfortable sharing that fact.

We are mindful of the "overplayed song syndrome." The more researchers and school leaders focus on self-efficacy, the more it seems to become like a favorite song. We all have favorite songs when they are first released, but after a while we hear them so many times, we begin to change the station or hide it on our playlist. Self-efficacy is at risk of suffering this fate. This would be unfortunate, as it explains so much of how people move in professional settings; it's all based in human behavior. Bandura (2010) writes,

> Human behavior is extensively motivated and regulated through the exercise of self-influence. Among the mechanisms of self-influence, none is more focal or pervading than belief in one's personal efficacy. (p. 179)

Internal self-awareness and external self-awareness play critical roles in shaping an individual's self-efficacy. Internal self-awareness involves a deep understanding of one's own strengths, weaknesses, values, and emotions. When individuals possess high levels of internal self-awareness, they can more accurately assess their competencies and limitations. This self-awareness allows them to set realistic goals and make effective plans to achieve them. Consequently, their self-efficacy tends to be higher, as they have confidence in their abilities and can channel their efforts effectively toward desired outcomes.

External self-awareness, on the other hand, pertains to one's ability to understand how others perceive them, including their strengths and weaknesses. This external perspective can be a valuable source of feedback and insights that can help individuals improve their self-efficacy. When people receive constructive feedback and validation from others, it can boost their confidence and belief in their abilities. Additionally, external self-awareness enables individuals to build a support network and seek assistance when needed, further enhancing their self-efficacy. In contrast, those who lack external self-awareness may struggle to gauge their true capabilities and may have difficulty mobilizing external resources, which can hinder their self-efficacy. Therefore, a balance of internal and external self-awareness is essential in nurturing and sustaining high levels of self-efficacy.

Intentional leadership is about understanding your strengths and areas of growth. It requires you to engage in situations that will help you learn how to strengthen your areas of weakness and learn from others. This is important because when it comes to self-efficacy, Bandura (2010) writes,

> When faced with obstacles, setbacks, and failures, those who doubt their capabilities slacken their efforts, give up, or settle for mediocre solutions. Those who have a strong belief in the capabilities redouble their effort to master the challenge. (p. 180)

One of the other reasons it is important for you to understand self-efficacy as a leader centers on how our self-efficacy can work against you. Bandura (2010) found that

> individuals who are highly assured in their capabilities and the effectiveness of their strategies are disinclined to seek discordant information that would suggest the need for corrective adjustments. (p. 183)

What this means is that confidence doesn't always equate to competence. Due to this aspect of self-efficacy, we are suggesting that self-awareness also means understanding one's confidence but being open to listening to dissenting opinions. The bottom line is that just because you think you are right doesn't always mean you are actually right.

We would like to give you some time to reflect on this topic of dissenting opinions and being open to listening, so please engage with the Leading With Intention deep reflection activity. The activity is meant to bring two different topics together. We want you to reflect on your leadership self-awareness, and we want you to reflect on whether you are comfortable with people who challenge you as a leader.

LEADING WITH INTENTION

Self-efficacy is the confidence we have in our actions. All of us, including the two of us authoring this book, have areas where we feel confident and areas where we don't. However, Bandura's (1997, 2010) research shows us that confidence is not enough, and that we must seek out "discordant information." You will notice a theme from our self-awareness conversation that surrounding ourselves with a diverse group of people who will disagree with us and "be real" is important. Take some time to consider the following:

- Who makes up your diverse group of people that will be real with you?

- How have they helped change your thinking?

- Consider one example of a situation where your level of confidence prevented you from asking the right questions because you thought you knew it all already?

- How might you move forward in your leadership practices knowing that confidence doesn't always mean competence?

Leadership self-awareness is not just about understanding how you lead and listen to those confidants that you keep close around you. Leadership self-awareness is about how you are open to the insight and opinions of those educators that you often find yourself disagreeing with as well. Why? Because educators who are disgruntled often are those who don't feel like their voices are valued. They feel less valued as time goes on. Those educators have something positive to offer you.

CONCLUSION

Sometimes you may believe you are fully self-aware, and then you have a person close to you give feedback that surprises you. The first Leading With Intention activity asked you to videotape yourself at a meeting or a professional learning session to see if your level of self-awareness matches up with how you really act. We don't intend this to create moments of self-judgment. Leaders have a tendency to judge themselves too harshly using their inner critical voice. What we want is for you to have insight into how you interact with others. Use that insight to help you improve; don't use it to judge yourself.

Understanding yourself as a leader gives you a window into your own self-efficacy, which is highly important. Every leader or educator needs to understand their areas of strength and areas of growth. What can make your life in education more fulfilling is to have something to focus and work on that will ultimately get you to meet that success criteria you set for yourself when it comes to leadership. Understanding self-awareness and self-efficacy provides you with an opportunity to connect with your staff, students, and community in deeper ways, which will enhance your leadership and practices. In the next chapter, we explore how to connect with your staff through the practice of human interconnectedness.

REFLECTION QUESTIONS

- How did this chapter make you feel?

- Why is self-awareness as a leader important?

- In what ways might you have an internal level of self-awareness but lack an external level of self-awareness?

- Self-efficacy is the confidence we have in our own actions. Where do you feel the greatest level of self-efficacy?

- We explored self-efficacy focusing on confidence, which doesn't always lead to competence. In what ways can you make sure you are focusing on both confidence and competence?

Now that you have read the chapter, take some time to consider what you have learned, and then think about how you learned it. Fill in the L and H sections of the KWLH chart. Did something we wrote align with actions you have taken? Did you take time away from reading the chapter and find yourself right in the middle of one of the situations we wrote about? You will continue to see the KWLH chart as we move through the book, so be prepared to start considering how you learned the information you learned.

HOW DID WE DO?

By the end of this chapter, you will have learned to

- Engage with a metacognitive strategy that will help activate prior knowledge

- Process the elements of leadership self-awareness and consider two or three actions you can take today

- Be able to name two categories of self-awareness and relate them to your own self-awareness

- Identify four archetypes of self-awareness and how they are related to context

- Identify how leadership self-efficacy impacts what we do as leaders

Self-Awareness KWLH Chart

Take some time to consider what you have learned after reading the chapter, and then think about how you learned it.

K	W	L	H
WHAT DO I KNOW?	WHAT DO I *WANT* TO LEARN?	WHAT HAVE I LEARNED?	*HOW* DID I LEARN IT?

Call to Action

Consider one of the strategies that we offered within the chapter (e.g., videotape yourself leading, use the habit tracker) and try it in the next week. Before you engage in the activity, consider the following questions.

- What do you want it to look like?

- What are you hoping to learn by engaging in it?

CHAPTER 2

Fostering Human Interconnectedness

What is essential is invisible to the eye.

—*The Little Prince* by Antoine de Saint-Exupéry

By the end of this chapter, you will

- Understand the definition and meaning of human connectedness

- Develop strategies for knowing yourself and others in developing human interconnectedness

- Acknowledge the ongoing impact of the COVID-19 pandemic on human interaction and connectedness

- Identify strategies for leadership that promote genuine interconnectedness with staff, students, and community

When you hear the phrase *human interconnectedness*, what do you believe you know about it? What would you like to learn?

HUMAN INTERCONNECTEDNESS
KWLH CHART

K	W	L	H
WHAT DO I *KNOW?*	WHAT DO I *WANT TO LEARN?*	WHAT HAVE I *LEARNED?*	*HOW* DID I LEARN IT?

By the end of this chapter, I want to...

-
-

HUMAN INTERCONNECTEDNESS

Human interconnectedness is fostered when the members of a community focus on open communication and honor the ability to respectfully challenge each other's thinking and beliefs, which results in a deeper and more intentional learning environment. In her journal article "The Persistence of Privacy: Autonomy and Initiative in Teachers' Professional Relations," Judith Warren Little (1990) writes,

> School teaching has endured largely as an assemblage of entrepreneurial individuals whose autonomy is grounded in norms of privacy and noninterference and is sustained by the very organization of teaching work. Teachers are now being pressed, invited, and cajoled into ventures in "collaboration," but the organization of their daily work often gives them scant reason for doing so. Long-standing occupational and organizational traditions, too, supply few precedents; rather, they buttress teaching as a private endeavor. (p. 530)

It's not just teachers who are being asked to engage in collaboration, but leaders are asked to do the same, both with other leaders and with their teachers as well.

As we prefaced in the opening of the book, we are approaching this book a bit differently than you may have experienced with other books. We include stories in each chapter because doing so conveys learning in other ways than focusing only on text and research. You are also being encouraged to share your story and think about the legacy you want to leave in education. We offer this researched-based practice through story because we know how stories can connect us. The stories you provide will show your experiences and how you approached issues that you faced, and ultimately how you took those issues to develop human interconnectedness.

Little (1990) writes, "The move from conditions of complete independence to thoroughgoing interdependence entails changes in the frequency and intensity of teachers' interactions, the prospects for conflict, and probability of mutual influence" (p. 512).

Developing human interconnectedness is a strength for Mike Nelson, and within this chapter we provide three stories from Mike that are tied to research and practice. The first story helps illustrate how the simplest of actions can engage people in the deepest of ways, and how other simple actions can prevent those connections from continuing.

 ## Knowledge Through Storytelling

The Road Ahead

In 1995, Bill Gates released the book *The Road Ahead*. I was in my third year as a building principal. At the time, I found reading the book was like reading a science fiction novel as Gates shared technological advances that would occur over the next decade. Many of the words he used were familiar, but the discussion was still difficult

for me to understand. The context for which these words were used was very unfamiliar. I needed to use every reading strategy I taught to my five- and six-year-old students to make meaning!

Gates (1995) pointed out the invention of the telephone as a major advancement in two-way communication over face-to-face conversations. He considered it more

(Continued)

(Continued)

efficient than face-to-face conversation as at the time "any good talk entailed a visit and probably a meal, and one could expect to spend a full afternoon or evening" (p. 3). He then went on to state, "As I write, a newer form of communication—electronic email, or e-mail—is undergoing the same sort of process; establishing its own rules and habits" (p. 3).

As a first-year principal in 1992, I used a communication strategy that my staff referred to as a "green book." This was simply a notebook filled with green copy paper. Each morning, I would handwrite a message to staff members about the day ahead, a quote from a book, a strategy to try, or simply a message to have a great day. The green book was placed on a table by itself. Sometimes next to the book there would be donuts, cookies, salty snacks, a new pen or pencil to use, or another offering. Each morning, staff would arrive and gather around the green book. Not only were they informed about the events of the school day; they also connected with each other on a personal and professional level. The green book served our school the way business staff in a company building might gather around the proverbial watercooler.

Not long after I read Gates's book, our school district purchased computers for each teacher. Gates (1995, p. 31), when describing

human behaviors and the acceptance of technological changes, used a quote from Antoine de Saint-Exupéry's 1939 memoir: "Little by little, the machine will become a part of humanity." As an early adopter of new technologies, I immediately saw the efficiency benefit of a staff email and began sending out a morning message via email rather than using the green book. Some staff loved it while others missed the green book. At the time, I was a young leader whose staff were older than I was. I shared the importance of embracing this new technology, particularly as educators, to remain current in these new experiences. Several staff members didn't want to open up their computer and read the daily email, but I didn't waiver. The green book went away. In reflection, many of the personal and professional connections staff had with each other every morning also went away.

The Road Ahead has remained on my bookshelf for almost three decades and has had an impact on my leadership. I recently read it again and found that I did not need to use any reading strategies to make meaning and understand its content. Not only did I understand it; I *lived* the experience that Gates told me I would so many years ago. The technology that Gates spoke about in the book in terms of the efficiencies of communication through email is a natural part of the work environment for educators.

Consider Mike's story and reflect on your own actions as a leader. Have you had a similar experience where you adopted what seemed to be a better strategy only to find that there was a downside to the decision?

LEADING WITH INTENTION

Mike was an early adopter of email. At the time, it was groundbreaking to be able to instantly communicate with others without leaving the desk. However, what he found was that the green book practice brought people together ... including people who had no other opportunity to interact during the day.

- Have you made a decision, which seemed like a good one, only to find out there were some undesirable consequences?
- What was the decision?
- What were the consequences?
- How did you overcome those consequences?
- What did you learn from the experience?

Mike's story highlights the importance of human connection and gathering with intentionality. Meetup is an online platform where people from around the world offer gatherings centered on a common purpose. That common purpose could be a running club, single people going for hikes, or a resource for those who want to learn how to paint using watercolors. The person creating the opportunity knows "the why" and uses it in their marketing, and those attending also know "the why," which is why they show up. Unfortunately, those elements are often missing in how we learn in our school communities, and unless we are self-aware, understand the need to connect with one another, and know our priorities as a school or district leader, those rare opportunities that we get to come together and learn from one another will be missed. The goal is for everyone to clearly know why they are in the room.

What Mike did with the green book in the faculty room was create a space for people to meet up, and they gravitated toward that experience. However, with email he was able to streamline how people communicated. But the streamlined process was missing some elements. Mike learned a lot from the experience and figured out other ways to bring people together. It was a good learning lesson for him, and one that he carried with him through his career.

Knowledge Through Storytelling (Continued)

Need for Connection

Looking back, even though sending out a staff email each morning was a more efficient manner to communicate the day's events at our school, it shifted the culture of our building. Without the green book, there was no longer a reason for every staff member to walk to the staff-room. Having incidental and collaborative conversations with other staff members about personal and professional topics diminished greatly. As a leader, I also found myself not regularly seeing staff members. And yet my one-way communication style (email) greatly increased. I just didn't know if it was being read or how people were reacting.

A Good Manager

1. Is a good coach
2. Empowers the team and does not micromanage
3. Expresses interest in and concern for team members' success and personal well-being
4. Is productive and results-oriented
5. Is a good communicator—listens and shares information
6. Helps with career development
7. Has a clear vision and strategy for the team
8. Has key technical skills that help them advise the team
9. **Collaborates across [the company]**
10. **Is a strong decision maker**

Other businesses and organizations experienced similar outcomes. In response, in the early 2000s they shifted to more open workspaces and included play areas and cafés as a way to spark needed collaboration and connection between employees and garner more productivity. In 2008, Google launched Project Oxygen to study the work environment they created and, as a result of the project, determined what makes a good manager. Take a look at the first eight attributes original to the 2008 study and then the ninth and tenth from the 2018 update.

Most of the attributes pertain to communication, connection, and relationships. Maggie Wooll (2022), in a blog post titled "Your Workforce Is Lonely. It's Hurting Your Business," states,

> The experience of connectedness is vital in our work lives. And not just because work is where people spend a significant chunk of time. We are beginning to recognize how connection affects individual and team-level trust, agility, and resilience. Ultimately, this impacts performance as well as an organization's ability to retain high-performing talent, solve complex challenges, and navigate tough times together.

In the same blog, Wooll asserts we have a connection crisis in the workforce that leaders have the leadership influence to address:

> When leaders make social connection an organizational priority—when it is rewarded and tracked like any other goal—and take active measures to facilitate it across the employee spectrum, performance, productivity and well-being go up, and talent stays.

WHAT'S YOUR STORY?

Write about an experience that you have had that is similar to Mike's story, or write about a time when you developed a strong connection with other colleagues when you didn't expect to.

The second story from Mike is about how we can foster inter-connectedness. While reading, pay attention to some of the actions the team took and how people felt. Perhaps you are a teacher or leader who doesn't need to kick off a two-year professional learning journey like the one Mike describes. But setting the environment for learning is something we all need to do.

Knowledge Through Storytelling

Shift From Relationships to Human Interconnectedness

Throughout my career, I have heard how important relationships are for students, staff, parents, and community. I have heard speakers receive standing ovations when they affirm that it is all about relationships. Everyone seems to be united in this. But it is often trivialized as buying donuts for your staff, sending a newsletter to parents, or greeting your students at the door. These are all good things, but they are one-sided. They describe the person in power doing something for others. These examples are also one size fits all in that everyone receives the same response or action from the leader.

In October 2021, the Washington Association of School Administrators (WASA) launched an initiative to work with all teaching and learning administrators across the state. As much as this might seem odd, this group had never been called to gather at a statewide level. It would also be the first in-person professional learning event following the shutting down of schools as a result of the coronavirus.

The launch occurred in a hotel ballroom set with round tables distanced according to health department standards. In the center of each table were different sizes of river rocks. Participants wondered about the rocks as they took their seats. The learning session began with the reading of the book *The Circles All Around Us* by Brad Montague (2021). The rocks symbolized how we are all circles. Throughout life experiences, our circles grow, ripple, and interconnect.

By the end of the book reading, the majority of participants' eyes were filled with tears. Those present shared, "I didn't realize how much I have missed being together," "These [meaning teaching and learning leaders] are my people," and "It's about relationships." Each person chose a rock symbolizing the leadership ripples each person can make when tossed in water. With many leaders and many rocks, ripples begin to overlap or interconnect.

As we reflect on these examples of the importance of relationships, a phrase comes to mind: *human interconnectedness*. Using the following Leading With Intention prompt, take some time to reflect on how you develop connections among staff and students. As you read on, keep your own story about developing connections among staff and students close to you so you can take what you learn from us and apply it to your own context.

LEADING WITH INTENTION

For full disclosure, Peter was not on board with reading a picture book at the beginning of a two-year kickoff event, but within moments of the book being read, he quickly changed his mind. After the reading, the demeanor of the whole audience shifted from anxious to relaxed and engaged.

When it comes to facilitating professional learning, running faculty meetings, or gathering as a school leadership team, how do you move beyond relationships and look for ways that you are truly interconnected? As a school leader, how do you foster interconnectedness?

WHY HUMAN INTERCONNECTEDNESS?

The media seems to tell us that we can all be superhuman—from how we look, to how we behave, to how we acquire wealth. As educational leaders, it is important for us to remain grounded in what makes us human and how collectively we can create better situations for our students and staff.

In an article written for the Dana Foundation, Michael Platt, PhD, states,

> Human beings are wired to connect—and we have the most complex and interesting social behavior out of all animals. This social behavior is a critical part of our adaptive toolkit. It allows us to come together and do things that we wouldn't be able to do on our own. We're only just beginning to uncover how these mechanisms may operate in real world activities, and the findings are really exciting.
>
> —(quoted in Wellington, 2021)

Unfortunately, our education system is full of silos whether you look at it through the lens of funding or programs or general structures of a school system. The key to breaking down these silos and achieving what Platt says of doing things (for students) that you wouldn't be able to do on your own is using the people within the school system who have a natural and innate desire to connect.

It's more than simply being connected. One can be connected, yet still remain a silo in the work. Principal teams can come together and connect on a regular basis yet walk away from these meetings and continue leading in the same silo of their school as before. But transformation happens when principal teams come together and fully recognize, acknowledge, and plan in a way where they need each other to fully perform at the highest level of interconnectedness. Interconnectedness occurs when there is reciprocity throughout the different levels of a school system.

The two words together, *human + interconnected*, can best be understood with the metaphor of the giant redwood tree. Redwood trees have a shallow root system. If they were to stand alone during turbulent times, they would easily topple over. But redwood trees growing and thriving together have an interconnected root system that allows them to flourish and thrive during turbulent conditions. A school system built on human interconnectedness will move beyond a one-size-fits-all relationship model and therefore better meet the needs of each student.

How would you describe human interconnectedness? Why is it important for leaders to possess this trait? What might be a barrier to it?

HUMAN INTERCONNECTEDNESS AND YOUR LEADERSHIP HEART

Toward the end of the book *The Leadership Challenge*, James Kouzes and Barry Posner (2023) quote former Seattle Public Schools superintendent John Stanford:

> The secret to success [in life] is to stay in love. Staying in love gives you the fire to ignite other people, to see inside other people, to have greater desire to get things done than other people. A person who is not in love doesn't really feel the kind of excitement that helps them to get ahead and to lead others and to achieve. I don't know any other fire, any other thing in life that is more exhilarating and is more positive a feeling than love is. (pp. 323–324)

Stanford knew himself and his leadership heart. A leadership heart is an internal moral compass for leading others. In Chapter 1, we explored the importance of becoming self-aware and intentional in your leadership actions and behavior. In this chapter, we are making the case that self-awareness and knowing your leadership heart are of critical importance when   of human interconnectedness. For leaders to   interconnectedness exists,   as leaders and know their   now their strengths and use   also know their weaknesses   n so that the rest of the team   rt the leader in an inter-

                                     d between authenticity and   as nouns. Jordan Harbinger   a noun to an adjective in this   ity means being open to other   yourself, simply because you   ersion of yourself." Harbinger   mean we need to embody or   ry single moment. There are contexts in which vulnerability is unnecessary, inappropriate, and sometimes even dangerous." We've seen a leader be too vulnerable, therefore losing credibility.

WHAT'S YOUR STORY?

Share your human interconnectedness story. Write about a time when you had to find a balance between vulnerability and authenticity because you were concerned you might lose credibility. What did you do?

We understand that finding authentic vulnerability is a struggle, so we are grateful if you provided an example. In this final story for the chapter, Mike shares a leadership moment where he was self-aware of his feelings and moved them forward in a positive way to model authentic vulnerability.

Knowledge Through Storytelling

A Leadership Move That Develops Empathy

If you're a school superintendent, many decisions fall on you. One decision that was always stressful for me was when to delay or close school due to inclement weather. Our district covered 440 square miles. When a winter weather storm occurred, it took several of us getting up at 3:30 in the morning to drive around the district to make a safety assessment. No matter what decision was made, I would spend the morning answering the phone, listening, and carefully responding to families. I had empathy for families because I knew that shifting day care plans quickly is difficult. On the other hand, if school remained open after a storm, I had empathy for parents who called expressing their concern for their high school–aged children who drove themselves to school.

One day my whole process regarding school closure decisions changed. A comment posted on social media read, "I bet he just stands on his porch and makes the decision about the safety of our students." This could not be further from the truth. In most situations I can make decisions quite quickly, but I agonized over the decision of whether it was safe for our bus drivers, staff, and students to arrive at school.

In the Myers–Briggs Type Indicator, I score as an extrovert, intuitive, feeler, and judger (ENFJ). I am high in the area of an intuitive feeler (NF). Obviously the comment about making the decision of declaring a snow day was bothersome. How could I use knowing myself to respond better in this example? I altered a couple of things. First, the decision for snow days came out in my voice. When families received the auto message, they heard directly from me about the conditions.

What the public didn't know was that my dog, Duncan, always came with me. Duncan loved to sleep, but he always awoke when he sensed it was a snow day. Together we would drive the roads, ultimately ending at Starbucks. Duncan wanted his "pup cup" of whipped cream. The second change I made was to begin snapping photos of Duncan and me when we stopped on the road, showing the weather conditions. Quickly this became known as the "Duncan Report." Our communications department created a Duncan Report image, and he became the natural spokesperson. The first time the Duncan Report went out with the decision about snow-related closures, something strange happened. I received no calls complaining about the decision.

Michael Grinder (2007), in his study of nonverbal communication, discusses that

(Continued)

(Continued)

when having an in-person conversation with another person you should sit at a 90° angle. He also suggested you have a third focal point in the room, usually a piece of paper listing key information. This subtle strategy moves the conversation from each other to the points on the paper, therefore allowing more collaboration and connection. Even though I was having a conversation with a few thousand families through phone calls and social media, I believe Duncan acted as the third point.

Duncan became a regular part of weather communication, and students, staff, and parents looked forward to "hearing" from him. If a weather storm was predicted, I would receive emails of care for Duncan's safety. I know they meant it for me, too, but I was never "called out." Since leaving the superintendency but still living in the same community, I am often asked about Duncan. Usually, the conversation starts with "We miss Duncan."

Think of a time when you experienced authentic vulnerability in a leader who was both self-aware and aware of their leadership heart. In the following Leading With Intention activity, reflect on how you responded when that leader showed vulnerability.

LEADING WITH INTENTION

How did you respond or react when a leader showed you authentic vulnerability?

Think of a time when you demonstrated authentic vulnerability. What was the response from your team?

Sometimes we get accused of focusing on the soft stuff when we talk about self-awareness, human interconnectedness, and vulnerability, but we believe this is the necessary work of leaders within school communities. It brings people together, helps them develop agency, and inspires innovation.

In addition to our belief in developing strong connections, we believe in strong self-responsibility. We believe that teachers, leaders, and staff are accountable for their actions. Being human with one another helps people lean into accountability as opposed to running away from it.

It seems like common sense that being genuine would be a natural part of building connections. Unfortunately, that is not always true. In our fast-paced world, where people are busy and we are checking our phones hundreds of times a day, we are at risk of trying to develop connectedness at the same time we try to check it off the list of "to-dos."

HUMAN INTERCONNECTEDNESS IS BEING GENUINE

The third element for a leader to consider when building a culture of human interconnectedness is being genuine. Psychologist Guy Winch (2015) offers three basic reasons why people are drawn to others who they perceive as being genuine:

1. We are much more likely to trust a genuine person than a fake one because we believe those who are true to themselves are also likely to be truer and more honest with *us*.
2. We often associate genuineness with appealing traits, such as strength of character and emotional resilience—and correctly so, as being true to yourself takes confidence, tenacity, and often bravery.
3. We are attracted to uniqueness and individuality, qualities genuine people usually have in spades.

Knowing that being genuine is one key attribute of building a culture of human interconnectedness, what are behaviors and actions that generate the feeling in others that you are being genuine? Winch (2015) has widely shared seven habits of truly genuine people as an answer to this question.

- Genuine people speak their minds.
- Genuine people respond to *internal* expectations, not *external* ones.
- Genuine people forge their own paths.
- Genuine people are not threatened by failure.
- Genuine people can admit their faults.
- Genuine people are not judgmental of others.
- Genuine people have solid self-esteem.

CONCLUSION

This chapter may seem a bit different in structure and language from the others. It is critical to us that when talking about human interconnectedness, we describe it through leadership stories in which you can visualize and feel.

Through the reading of stories, our hope is that you are able to experience deep leadership in recognizing that human interconnectedness.

There has always been a need for leaders to build relationships with those whom they lead. Relationships alone can still have the culture of an organization missing critical elements of connection. Only through human interconnectedness can a school can thrive and flourish for its students.

REFLECTION QUESTIONS

- Name three attributes about yourself that you believe support building a culture of human interconnectedness.
- Name three attributes about yourself that you don't believe support building a culture of human interconnectedness. How can being self-aware of these attributes help you become a stronger leader?
- How would the people you lead describe how you contribute to building human interconnectedness to support staff learning and student achievement?
- Who is a leader that you feel is genuine and has developed human interconnectedness with the people they lead? What behaviors and actions do they exhibit that demonstrate human interconnectedness? Ask them to share with you their list about themselves. Compare their list with what you wrote. How do they differ? How are they the same?

HOW DID WE DO?

By the end of this chapter, you will have learned to

- Understand the definition and meaning of human connectedness
- Develop strategies for knowing yourself and others in developing human interconnectedness
- Acknowledge the ongoing impact of the COVID-19 pandemic on human interaction and connectedness
- Identify strategies for leadership that promote genuine interconnectedness with staff, students, and community

Human Interconnectedness KWLH Chart

Take some time to consider what you have learned after reading the chapter, and then think about how you learned it.

K	W	L	H
WHAT DO I KNOW?	WHAT DO I *WANT TO LEARN?*	WHAT HAVE I LEARNED?	*HOW* DID I LEARN IT?

Call to Action

Consider one of the strategies that we offered within the chapter (e.g., setting the environment, using picture books) and try it in the next week. Before you engage in the activity, consider the following questions.

- What do you want it to look like?
- What are you hoping to learn by engaging in it?

CHAPTER 3

Collective Inquiry

By the end of this chapter, you will

- Engage in the four steps of the collective inquiry process
- Make connections between self-awareness, human interconnectedness, and the priorities leaders establish for their schools or districts
- Define four types of evidence that will help evaluate impact as well as establish areas of focus

In Chapter 1, we engaged you in learning around leadership self-awareness and self-efficacy, and then in Chapter 2 we explored the importance of fostering human interconnectedness, as well as how to develop it within our school communities. All of this enhances how you engage with those you work with in your school or district. This chapter will focus on how leadership self-awareness, human interconnectedness, and the desire to engage with intentionality can help you lead to school improvement, and for that we will explore the use of collective inquiry.

Collective inquiry is a research-based method for attaining improvement in our practices. The goal of this chapter is to use the research around self-awareness, self-efficacy, and human interconnectedness, as well as the practices you have read through stories and strategies in Chapters 1 and 2, to help guide you through some of the priorities you may be working on in your building or district leadership position.

Let's begin with what you know, and what you want to learn, about collective inquiry.

COLLECTIVE INQUIRY KWLH CHART

K	W	L	H
WHAT DO I KNOW?	WHAT DO I *WANT TO LEARN?*	WHAT HAVE I LEARNED?	*HOW* DID I LEARN IT?

By the end of this chapter, I want to...

•

•

From the stories we have offered, you probably are getting a sense of who we are as humans and leaders. Both of us have a need to go deeper each and every time we engage in coaching, workshops, and conference sessions. The two of us interact, as co-teachers, before, during, and after those sessions because we do not just want to be well planned and thoughtful in our approach; we also want to be flexible enough that we can change course if necessary based on the needs of the learners before us.

Recently, we have been asking our audiences to ponder legacy. We know this is a big question, but when you have a strong level of self-awareness and want to develop stronger connections, you are not just working on the day-to-day actions but are also creating a legacy that you will one day leave behind. This has everything to do with collective inquiry and your priorities as a leader because it makes the difference between being remembered as just a good manager and being remembered as a leader who valued learning and growth.

In the following story, Mike shares an example of how he added to his legacy as an instructional leader and intentionally helped others engage in a cycle of improvement.

Knowledge Through Storytelling

Deeply Knowing Others and Honoring Their Values

Have you ever had a leadership experience where you weren't necessarily set up for success? For me, that experience came after several years as a principal in a large urban district south of Seattle. The school where I served as principal had just been recognized as a National Blue Ribbon School by the U.S. Department of Education—mostly due to our reading achievement at all grade levels placing us in the second position of all elementary schools behind a school with less than 10% poverty. Our poverty level, in contrast, was one of the highest in the district. A week after this recognition, which received some significant press, the superintendent moved me to become principal of an elementary school with the lowest reading scores. The superintendent in the paper stated that I would change student performance in reading within two years and that he had shifted my title to Reading Czar. Even writing this now, I can feel my heart begin to race.

Luckily for me, he made this decision several months before the end of the school year. What I chose to do during these months was not what the superintendent thought I should be doing, but he gave me the freedom to lead in the way I felt was best. Staff members and parents knew about the reading scores of their students, but because the shift in leadership happened so abruptly, the story received local and regional news coverage. The school community was not used to having the dismal scores shared so publicly. They also were not excited about having a "fixer" brought in.

Over the course of the first months, I used several strategies to overcome the fixer connotation, but the most public one—and the one I believe had the most impact—had me going into fifth-grade classrooms several times a week. These students would soon begin the sixth grade, the highest grade in the school, and thus become the leaders of the school during my first year as principal.

During my first few visits, I would read aloud picture books about plants and gardens. Together we created charts of what we learned. I always left the classroom asking questions like "I wonder what the native plants of the region are" or "I wonder if anyone has a connection to a nursery or a landscaper." Without exception, the next time I came into the room, the students had answers to or thoughts about my previous questions. We captured this on charts and invited a few guest speakers.

After a few weeks, I brought in a large photo of the front of the school and asked what they thought. Their first answers were "It rocks!" and "We are the best!" When I asked them what they didn't see, the students began to say, "There are no plants or trees" and "The grass is dying." A student whose cousin went to a neighboring school, which had a lot of plants, wondered why our school did not have very good landscaping. It was a glorious moment. I had become part of the "we."

(Continued)

(Continued)

They wanted to do something. The students wrote letters to local nurseries, tree farms, and rock and gravel companies, seeking donations. I told them they needed to deliver a presentation to the head of the school district facilities department to ask for permission. The students did it all.

Parents began to hear about this idea, and they joined in and helped to plan. On the day of the project, nearly all students were accompanied by a family member eager to work with us. The plan was that everything would be delivered and we would transform the entrance to the school in one day, and that's exactly what happened. On the same day, one of the student committees for the project ran a learning session for each kindergarten through fourth-grade classroom about the project and took them on a tour of the worksite. The school district community was in awe of what the students accomplished in a single day.

We took photos of the event, and close to the end of the year, the fifth graders again shared how they completed the project with reading and research in a whole-school assembly. They ended the assembly with a wondering and a challenge of what each student might want to study over the summer. The students also announced that our school library would be open twice each week. The sixth graders, leaders of our school, led our reading initiative that spring and summer. Within a short period of time, we became known as the reading school. And yes, scores rose significantly in two years.

A week after the project, the superintendent called me into his office and said while he appreciated the upgrade to the entrance of the school, he didn't understand its connection to reading. I shared that I thought it had everything to do with reading (a slight exaggeration). I could have easily shared data with staff with an ultimatum that things needed to change, but the staff and parents already knew the data. That approach would not have built a true culture of learning. Human interconnectedness occurs when a leader knows their staff and understands their values. When leaders do the work of human interconnectedness, the people around them are more likely to lean in rather than lean away.

Mike's engaging stories throughout this chapter show how he modeled what we are writing about when it comes to human interconnectedness. Whether it's creating a school garden, building a new playground (which Peter did with his community), or getting people to shift their mindsets about reading scores and look at the bigger picture of supporting values of others while focusing on reading, we know you have stories of human interconnectedness and positive change.

WHAT'S YOUR STORY?

Think of a time when you watched a leader navigate an uncomfortable situation where they may not have been set up for success. What did they do well? What do you think they should have done differently?

Think of a time when you, as a leader, were put in an uncomfortable situation. What was your response? Like Mike, how did you go from *I* to *we*?

COLLECTIVE INQUIRY PROCESS

Self-awareness as a leader; understanding that self-efficacy is context specific, which can prevent us from focusing on places we find uncomfortable; and the importance of human interconnectedness can take us away from contrived collaboration (Little, 1990) to more impactful methods of authentic collaboration. Collective inquiry can help you solidify that interconnectedness, because when you do it well you can learn from those you work with and they will learn from you, which helps elevate your self-efficacy and increases your level of self-awareness.

Consider what you have learned from this book so far and how you might use collective inquiry to help you find more impact when it comes to your own self-awareness and how you foster human interconnectedness. Leadership centers on how you serve others and how you raise up the people around you. With that in mind, look at Figure 3.1, the Collective Inquiry Cycle Placemat. Get a sense of the exploration questions, which ask for your main priorities. You can focus on one, two, or three priorities based on your needs, but the goal is to not list more than three priorities.

Your one to three main priorities as a leader should be inspired by questions you have based on student evidence that explores a gap, a deficit, or an area of growth. Questioning your impact and using evidence to guide you is an important part of the inquiry process. Leo Casey (2014) writes, "Questions are the root of inquiry; they initiate, sustain, and invigorate each aspect of the process. Questions direct investigation, drive creativity, stimulate discussion, and are the bed-rock of reflection" (p. 510).

We find in our work, especially when we ask leaders to consider their priorities, that those leaders often have the same priorities they had the year before, and the year before that. Presently, some of this is due to COVID-19 and how slowly you may have come back from remote learning. Or it may be due to you taking the same action year after year, expecting different results. We do not mean for that to sound judgmental. In our work, we have seen leaders focus on the same priorities but not change any of the ways in which they try to achieve those priorities, because they don't take time to understand the evidence of impact of those actions.

Casey (2014) also found that, "when we describe learning in terms of inquiry, we are clearly affirming that learning and

FIGURE 3.1 ● Collective Inquiry Cycle Placemat

1. Problem of Practice		3. Evaluation	
What are up to three main priorities as a school/district? 1. _____ 2. _____ 3. _____	**What are your success criteria?** 1. _____ 2. _____ 3. _____ • **If you do this with intentionality, what will success look like?**	**What is your evidence of impact?** _____ _____ _____ (e.g., demographic, perceptions, student learning, or school processes; Bernhardt, 2018)	**Evidence Source 1** (Related to student learning; need identified in academic plan) _____ _____ _____
• **What is your evidence saying about your school/district and student growth and achievement?** • What does your academic plan or strategic plan focus on? • Are your priorities focused on the adults in the school, or are they focused on students? • How do they focus on equity and inclusion?	**What are your intended outcomes?** • _____ • _____ • _____ • _____	**Evidence Source 2** (Related to student learning; need identified in academic plan) _____ _____ _____ • Demographic data • Perceptions data • Student learning data • School processes data	**Evidence Source 3** (Related to teachers' and leaders' own learning) _____ _____ _____
2. Implementation		**4. Reflection and Next Steps**	
What is your working theory of action? _____ _____ _____ • **Think of this as an if–then statement.** *If* **you engage in these actions,** *then* **what are you expecting or hoping will happen?**	**Intentional Implementation** 1. Have you created a logic model? 2. What learning moves (activities) will you make? 3. What is your timetable? 4. What impact are you hoping to have on students, teachers, and leaders? 5. What will go on your "Not to Do" list? That is, what activities do you engage in that distract your focus or are no longer necessary (de-implementation)?	1. What did you learn while engaging in this cycle? 2. How did this impact students in a positive way? 3. What improvements did you make to your practice? 4. What did you stop doing so you can have more room to focus on what matters? 5. What would you do differently next time?	

questioning processes are somehow intertwined" (p. 510). This is why we are providing you with research, stories, and practice at the same time we want you to ponder questions about how you engage in this work.

INQUIRY: THREE PRIORITIES

We expect that this process will need to be broken down. We want you to explore your most important priorities and see where your own self-awareness and developing connections in your school community might help. Virtually every problem you face as a leader will take self-awareness to understand what actions you have taken to try to solve your issue, and what actions you need to continue to solve those issues. Those problems you face also take human interconnectedness, because schools are a human business, and only adults who feel connected to their leaders, school, and the work they do in school are going to give their very best.

Having said all that, you can explore this chapter in a variety of ways:

- Work on this section on your own, to see what the process is like (and then use the process with a team)
- Work on this section as a leadership team
- Use this section and process with a team of teachers or your faculty

Ultimately, when we engage in cycles of inquiry focused on school improvement, we should never do it alone, and this process should challenge our thinking and the thinking of others around us. We don't want this to be contrived collaboration, because not only is that far removed from the themes of this book, which focus on being intentional and connecting, but it is also a waste of time that will result in little impact on student learning. Judith Warren Little (1990) writes,

> Patterns of interaction that support mutual assistance or routine sharing may account well for maintaining a certain level of work-force stability, teacher satisfaction, and a performance "floor." They seem less likely, however, to account for high rates of innovation or for high levels of collective commitment to specific curricular or instructional policies. They seem less likely to force teachers' collective confrontation with the school's fundamental

purposes or with the implications of the pattern of practices that have accumulated over time. (p. 530)

This leads to your top three priorities. Your priorities as a school or district should be based on the following needs:

- They are connected to the district vision and mission.
- They are based on evidence (e.g., demographic, student learning, perceptions, and school processes data).
- They are priorities where your teachers and staff have capacity to engage in the work.
- They are balanced between an adult focus, like strengthening professional learning communities (PLCs), and a student learning need, like increasing proficiency rates in literacy.

Let's take a moment here for a Leading With Intention section to provide examples of how a leadership team can define their priorities together.

LEADING WITH INTENTION

- Using a protocol for learning (e.g., Five Whys, described in Figure 3.2), a school or district leadership team takes time to understand what their student learning evidence is telling them. Tease out where there might be deficits or areas of growth.

- Spend a sufficient amount of time (determined by the team) engaging in dialog about the most important priority areas.

- For some teams, this may take two or three meetings, but it should always include evidence (demographic, student learning, perceptions, and school processes data).

In order to have the discussions needed to get to the most important priorities, you can see where developing human interconnectedness is vital to the process. Recently, Peter attended a coaching session with an assistant superintendent in California who remarked how powerful he thought the questions guiding the priority section were, and wanted to make sure the building leaders he worked with were using them. The questions he referenced are as follows:

- What is your evidence saying about your school and student growth and achievement?
- What does your academic plan or strategic plan focus on?

- Are your priorities focused on the adults in the school, or are they focused on students?
- How do they focus on equity and inclusion?
- Take some time to write down two or three priorities.

In particular, the assistant superintendent pointed out this question as the most powerful: "Are your priorities focused on the adults in the school, or are they focused on students?" (We are not suggesting an area of focus can't involve adults. We just want to make sure that the area of focus concerning adults ultimately will impact students in a positive way.)

What two or three priorities are you working on for which you need the best thinking of the adults in your school or district? What deficit areas need your attention when it comes to students or adults?

The following are real examples of priorities from leaders that need the best thinking on the part of all adults:

- Increase the literacy proficiency rate of students
- Increase the use of active reading and reading instruction schoolwide
- Support PLC leads in building collective efficacy and being facilitators in increasing student achievement
- Support PLC to improve instruction/learning
- Reduce the number of suspension and discipline issues
- Improve attendance

List one, two, or three priorities you are focusing on in your school or district.

After defining one, two, or three priorities, teams may want to engage in a protocol like the one in Figure 3.2, the Five Whys for Inquiry.

The Five Whys for Inquiry protocol will help you solidify that the priorities are the correct focus, which is needed before moving on to the next step of developing success criteria. Recently, as co-facilitators of a workshop in the state of Washington for district leaders and their leadership teams, we used the Five Whys for Inquiry protocol to help teams see whether they had chosen the right priorities. Due to time constraints, we asked the teams to just focus on their first priority. We found the following successes and challenges:

- A couple of teams quickly engaged in the Five Whys for Inquiry protocol and got to the heart of their true priority.

FIGURE 3.2 ● The Five Whys for Inquiry

The Five Whys for Inquiry
Developed by the National School Reform Faculty
Purpose To help teams get at the foundational root of their priorities/inquiry question and to uncover multiple perspectives.
Presentation (3 minutes) The presenter describes the context of their priorities/inquiry. This might include why you selected the priority, why it's important to you, and how it relates to your school improvement work.
Clarifying Questions (2 minutes) The group asks clarifying questions. These questions can be answered with brief statements that clarify the context of the presenter's remarks.
Discussion (2 minutes) The group discusses the best line of inquiry to get at the heart of a "why" question and decides upon the initial "why" question. The presenter is silent.
"Why" Questioning (5–7 minutes) The "why" question that was decided upon is asked, and the presenter responds. Another "why" question is asked in response to the presenter's answer. This continues with a maximum of five "why" questions being asked.
Discussion (3 minutes) The group then discusses what they have heard the presenter say. Their discussion is not about solving a problem but an attempt to help the presenter understand the underlying causes for the issue they described. The presenter is silent.
Response (2 minutes) The presenter responds to what has been said. The group is silent.
Debrief (2 minutes) The group and presenter debrief the process.

- Some teams struggled to come up with the first "why" question. They spent so much time on the first "why" question that they did not have time for others.

One of the reasons one team struggled is they kept thinking about their challenges, so we needed to regroup and allow them more time, reassuring them that we would explore the challenges as well. This is a cautionary tale for you if you plan on using this protocol—we suggest you make sure to stay attentive to the fact that the "why" questions are focused on priorities and understand that the discussion about challenges needs time as well.

For the discussion about challenges, we used another protocol, loosely called the Realm of Concern (see Figure 3.3). The Realm of Concern protocol will help you define your success criteria, the next step in the process.

DEVELOPING SUCCESS CRITERIA

Step 1: In the Realm of Concern protocol, teams need to consider their main priority and engage in a conversation about the challenges they face when it comes to achieving that priority. Each member of the team takes sticky notes and writes down challenges—one for each sticky note. This process can take up to 20 minutes.

Step 2: The next step in the process is to engage in a group discussion to consider all the challenges and move those they believe they have influence (not control) over to the inner circle, or Realm of Influence. This process can take up to 30 minutes. One interesting outcome of the activity is to notice those challenges that the group doesn't think they have influence over. We have seen both leaders and teachers say that student engagement is a challenge, but not move it to the Realm of Influence.

Step 3: The last step in the process is to ask participants to move two or three of the challenges they believe they have influence over to the middle of the concentric circle. We then ask the participants to consider how these challenges can help them develop success criteria. As you can imagine, this activity takes a great deal of trust, which is why developing human interconnectedness is so important.

Think of developing success criteria as the qualitative aspect of reaching your goals. It might take your leadership team a full meeting to define those criteria, but using the Realm of

FIGURE 3.3 ● Realm of Concern

1. List the concerns you are hoping your priorities will address on sticky notes.
2. Place each one in the Realm of Concern.
3. Move the concerns within your influence to the Realm of Influence.
4. Move the concerns you have most influence over to the center circle, which we call the Realm of Decision-Making, because we want you to use those concerns as your starting point to define success criteria.

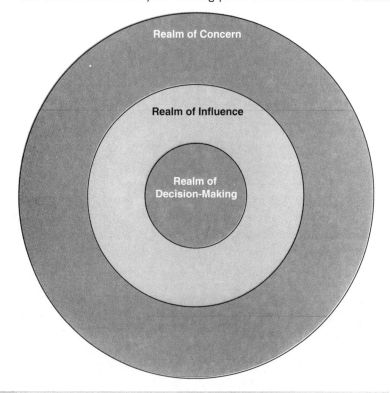

Concern protocol helps teams develop a great deal of intentionality ahead of time. Developing success criteria is important because it often helps deepen the language around the chosen priorities, and if leaders can clearly articulate a focus, then they are more likely to be able to continually communicate it to the school community. Success criteria are best when they lay out a process and not just a product (Clarke, 2021). When a leader who wrote that they wanted to improve attendance, for example, met with the two of us to find more intentional language, this is what we came up with:

By the end of this inquiry cycle, we will be able to

- Learn together how to better engage our students socially and emotionally and elevate their voices in the classroom
- Effectively develop an internal as well as external level of self-awareness
- Model metacognitive processes for staff
- Engage in conversations and actions with educators, students, and families that will result in stronger interconnections that will help improve school climate and culture
- Challenge educators to continually reexamine the extent to which their practices support the learning of all their students

WHAT'S YOUR STORY?

Take some time to write out your success criteria.

Your priorities and success criteria will lead to outcomes, which make up the more quantitative side of the story. What outcomes do you expect to happen? At this point, a team needs to go back to their evidence. Some examples of outcomes are as follows:

- We will see an increase in the number of students engaging in after-school activities, clubs, or schoolwide events due to our work on school climate, which will increase student attendance to 90%.

- We will see 100% of our PLCs engaging in cycles of inquiry.

 Write down the outcomes you expect to see if you achieve your priorities.

Priorities are nothing without implementation. In Mike's story from the beginning of the chapter, he made a conscious decision to implement literacy practices using a variety of strategies. He read to the students, helped increase engagement by asking them for their feedback, and used the feedback to foster a caring environment for students. Mike's story is a great example of fostering student engagement, the ultimate outcome when considering any priority. When students are proud of their environment and see that the adults around them care about them, they are more likely to increase engagement in their school. Theophilus Odetola (1972) and his colleagues found that students disengage from school because they (a) lack an emotional connection to their teacher or school community and (b) feel they do not have a voice in their own learning.

IMPLEMENTATION

Implementation is not a strong suit for many of us, so beginning an inquiry with a theory of action always helps. Jenni Donohoo (2013) writes, "Theories of action come in two types: espoused theories (stated as beliefs and values) and theories-in-use (actual behavior)" (p. 27). Defining a theory of action will take time, which may involve writing a rough-draft version and then rewriting until you get it right.

Before we ask you to write a working theory of action focused on your priorities, we would like to provide some examples for you. To give you some context, we used the following theory of action consistently in our work with the Washington Association of School Administrators' Instructional Leadership Network.

In this example, which was our espoused theory, we were helping directors of teaching and learning understand how to be more intentional with their implementations. Initiatives often fall short because educators don't recognize an issue in the first place, or they don't take enough time to focus on the knowledge, understanding, and skills to do the work. This book is about becoming more intentional by being more self-aware of your knowledge, understanding, and skills as a leader, as well as the knowledge, understanding, and skills of teachers and staff.

If you look at your beliefs and your actions, you will find times when your actions do not line up with your beliefs.

If we can develop a common language and common understanding about what authentic learning experiences mean, *then* teachers will develop a more consistent method of engaging students authentically.

If we want leaders and teachers in our district to possess the necessary understanding, knowledge, and skills to impact student learning, *then* we as directors of teaching and learning need to focus on the necessary understanding, knowledge, and skills needed to do that work.

Assumptions

- Leaders/teachers want our help.
- Leaders/teachers know there is an issue.
- We understand the necessary understanding, knowledge, and skills needed to help them.

Actions

- Offer effective professional learning
- Engage participants in the discussion before, during, and after

For example, you may believe that you develop connections with your staff by sending out a Sunday letter, but after you become more self-aware of what connections you want to make, you realize that your communication is usually one-sided. It focuses on what you as a leader want staff to know, without always including them in the process.

We want to share a story from Mike to help illustrate what we mean by our beliefs and actions. This story describes a big genuine action (clearly visible). After you read about the big action, Mike will share what he believes to be some of the micro genuine actions.

Knowledge Through Storytelling

The Sunday Evening News

More than a decade ago, the television show *Undercover Boss* became a phenomenon across the United States as company CEOs would disguise themselves and go undercover within their company. They would uncover employees doing amazing things to support the vision of the company. The show intrigued me, but it also caused me anxiety when watching as I wanted the featured employee to always do the right thing!

As a superintendent, I spent one spring playing the *Not-So-Undercover Boss*. I would spend a day truly working with various departments. I wanted to genuinely learn from each department and hear their values about the work they do. Here is an example of my Sunday Evening News, a letter I wrote to each staff member every week.

Sunday Evening News

How many of you have had the chance to watch the television show *Undercover Boss*?

I watched it for the first time two weeks ago. For the next several weeks, I will be doing a series in the Sunday Evening News titled *Not-So-Undercover Boss*.

This week, I had the incredible opportunity to spend a day with our amazing grounds crew.

I arrived bright and early in the grounds office located in a building within the transportation department. This group of five takes care of all the grounds at all our buildings. They also maintain their own equipment. In the past, this was contracted out, but doing this work in-house and owning our equipment was the fiscally responsible decision to make. The crew meets each day to quickly review the spring sports schedules.

In addition to general maintenance, our grounds crew is responsible for preparing all athletic fields. On this day—I was *so* lucky that it was beautifully sunny!—one was on his way to Black Diamond, another needed to prepare Osborne Field, and one needed to mow the soccer field.

(Continued)

(Continued)

Before we left the office, we chatted about their work. I wish you all could have been a part of this conversation. Here's some fun information:

- The crew uses a shop vacuum to remove puddles from baseball fields. They then apply "quick dry" to help absorb excess water. This helps prevent games from being postponed.

- The crew tests fields for pH levels each year. This year, the fields needed lime.

- When the crew fertilizes the fields, they fill a hopper with 450 pounds of fertilizer. It takes five hoppers to fertilize a field.

- The crew conducts their own research and development. They came up with a new and efficient way to collect and load leaves from our many deciduous trees on our properties.

- One of the crew is known as the satellite office on wheels as he travels to various sites beyond our major grounds.

The grounds crew also shared three things:

1. They keep track of how much change they find. Everyone says Tom is the best at finding coins. While we were together, one member found a dime!

2. They have the most amazing collection of small toys and army characters found on our fields exquisitely arranged on a shelf. I think it is a piece of art.

3. They keep track of how many moles they find and where they find them.

As we moved out to work, my assignment was to learn how to run a mower and then mow the soccer field. I first had to drive it down McDougall and then onto the field. I waved to a few parents along the way, who did some double takes. My dream (really a nightmare) during the night had been "Superintendent runs mower into car." Because of the teaching of our crew, I was able to maneuver the mower up and down the field . . . slowly at first and then a bit faster. I felt quite confident until I got too close to the soccer goal and had to back up, as I didn't know how to put the mower in reverse. Seeing that I was stuck, one crew member got in his golf cart to help me, but before he made it to the halfway line, I figured it out and managed to take the mower back down the field.

After mowing for a bit, the crew member took over and trained me in how to line the field. A large machine contains environmentally friendly paint in a ratio of two parts water to one part paint. Our crew takes such pride in lining our fields for our students. I *really* didn't want to mess this up. Thanks to expert guidance from the crew, I was able to use the machine somewhat successfully. I am quite proud of my lines!

I am so thankful for the opportunity to spend time with our amazing grounds crew. Two final quotes from crew members:

We have fun here, Mike.

Patience + Persistence = Progress

I asked our grounds crew to write a response to training me this week so you could hear their perspective. I am very appreciative of the words. I wasn't quite expecting this response, but it is what they sent me.

It has always been apparent that Mike Nelson is a "people person." The entire grounds crew is very appreciative that, as busy as Mike is, he recently spent a morning with us learning what we do for the district as well as letting us get to know him better. He came to the grounds department appropriately dressed and prepared to work—and he did just that. He was not afraid to get his hands dirty. Using the big mower, he did a splendid job of mowing the soccer field. He then painted the white lines on the field like a pro—his lines were even straight. Mike can work for us anytime.

Thank you, Mike, for being such a caring person. It was exciting and fun to have you visit. You have an invitation to stop by anytime.

—The grounds crew

The spring that I worked in every department was a magnificent learning time for me, and the sharing of my experiences in weekly letters to all staff and community brought a better understanding of the complexities of a school system. There was a sense of disbelief that I would take the time to engage in this experience. It was wonderful for me to walk in on staff and community members talking about the *Not-So-Undercover Boss* stories. I believe the stories of these experiences rippled so widely because of the genuine micro actions. Here are examples of what I mean:

- I arrived early for each experience. There is a perception that leaders are busy and thus given the OK to arrive late.

- I spent the day. I did not have a designated ending time of when I needed to leave.

- I dressed appropriately for the experience. I was known as "Suit Guy" in our school district, but I did not show up in a suit when I worked with the grounds department.

- The department led the conversation and the duties for the day. I became a team member for the day and let them lead me.

- I attempted to do what Zen Master Thich Nhat Hanh would describe as a deeply listening and loving speech. It's hard to find a person who doesn't want to feel their work is making a difference in some way. Honoring came naturally.

- *I modeled courage. I tried everything I was taught. I wasn't afraid to fail even though I was the superintendent.*

Mike knew that if he spent a day working with the grounds crew and highlighted it through his Sunday Evening News, he would not only be helping to elevate the voices of staff within the school community, but also be aligning his beliefs and actions. This was not a simple one-off that Mike did but a regular practice in his school leadership.

WHAT'S YOUR STORY?

Here's your opportunity to write your working theory of action. Take your time.

Now that you have outlined your three priorities, as well as the success criteria, outcomes, and working theory of action, it's time to talk about evaluation of impact. The next step in the collective inquiry process is collecting and looking at evidence to use to change our practices.

EVALUATION

Using Victoria Bernhardt's (2018) *Data Analysis for Continuous School Improvement*, you will see in Figure 3.4 the different types of evidence that can be collected to understand our impact.

Demographic data: Bernhardt suggests that school leaders not just look at their demographic data to understand their student population but use those data to look for areas of improvement.

Perceptions data: With perceptions data, you can use Mike's story from earlier to suggest surveying staff and students regarding school climate. The one issue to keep in mind is that school leaders often survey staff and students, but they are not intentional with what they learn. Do you do the same? Surveying staff means not just putting out results, but intentionally using those results to highlight possible improvement being pursued in the district.

Student learning data: Schools using common formative assessments (CFAs) can use those data under the concept of assessment *for* learning, but only when teachers are using that information to adjust teaching and learning in their classrooms. Additionally, CFAs can be used to address assessment *as* learning, but only if teachers are working side by side with students to help balance the power structure between teachers and students. Assessment *of* learning is the typical state assessment or standardized testing data.

School processes data: As you can see from Figure 3.4, school processes data are where processes like school leadership teams and PLCs, as well as programs, enter the equation.

To further illustrate the use of evidence and the evolution that schools can go through when processing the different types, Figure 3.5 outlines five overarching questions:

1. Where are we now?
2. How did we get to where we are?
3. Where do we want to be?

FIGURE 3.4 ● Multiple Measures of Data

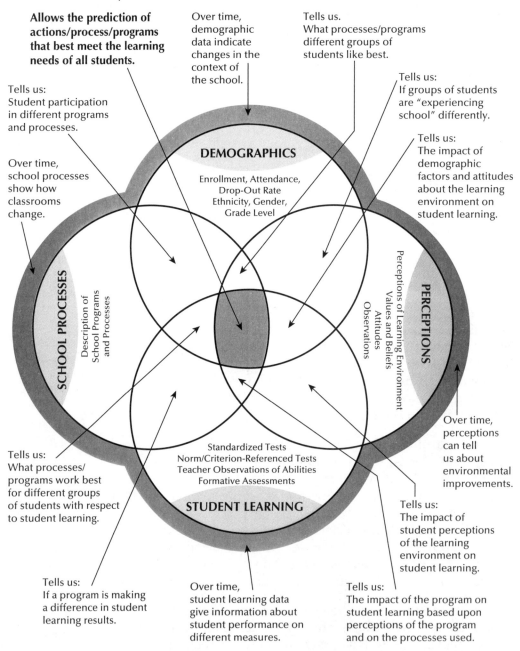

Allows the prediction of actions/process/programs that best meet the learning needs of all students.

Over time, demographic data indicate changes in the context of the school.

Tells us. What processes/programs different groups of students like best.

Tells us: Student participation in different programs and processes.

Tells us: If groups of students are "experiencing school" differently.

Over time, school processes show how classrooms change.

Tells us: The impact of demographic factors and attitudes about the learning environment on student learning.

DEMOGRAPHICS

Enrollment, Attendance, Drop-Out Rate Ethnicity, Gender, Grade Level

SCHOOL PROCESSES

Description of School Programs and Processes

PERCEPTIONS

Perceptions of Learning Environment Values and Beliefs Attitudes Observations

Over time, perceptions can tell us about environmental improvements.

Tells us: What processes/ programs work best for different groups of students with respect to student learning.

Standardized Tests Norm/Criterion-Referenced Tests Teacher Observations of Abilities Formative Assessments

STUDENT LEARNING

Tells us: The impact of student perceptions of the learning environment on student learning.

Tells us: If a program is making a difference in student learning results.

Over time, student learning data give information about student performance on different measures.

Tells us: The impact of the program on student learning based upon perceptions of the program and on the processes used.

Source: Bernhardt (2018).

FIGURE 3.5 ● Continuous School Improvement Framework

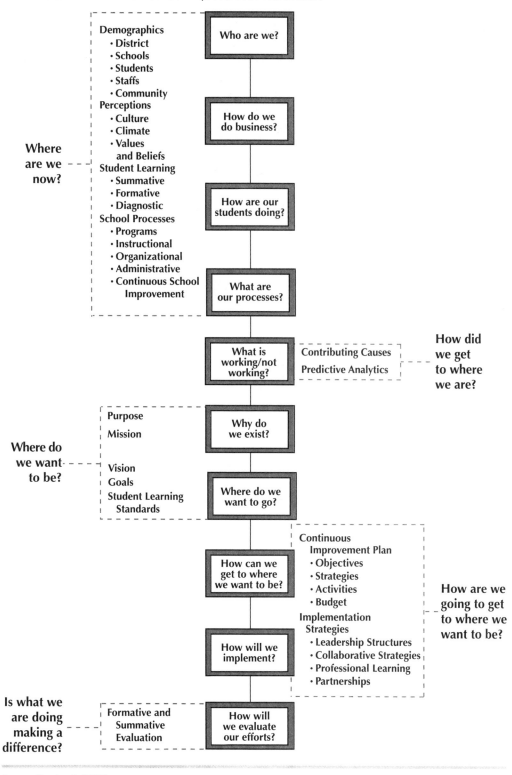

Source: Bernhardt (2018).

4. How are we going to get to where we want to be?

5. Is what we are doing making a difference?

On the notes page that follows, list your priorities, and then look back to Bernhardt's work as a reference. What evidence did you use to help you focus on each as a priority, and what evidence might you use to evaluate your impact? We have also added a section where you can write down how often you might progress monitor as a team.

Priority 1: _____

What evidence did you use to come to this conclusion?

What evidence will you use to evaluate impact?

How often will you progress monitor with the team?

Priority 2: _____

What evidence did you use to come to this conclusion?

What evidence will you use to evaluate impact?

How often will you progress monitor with the team?

Priority 3: _____

What evidence did you use to come to this conclusion?

What evidence will you use to evaluate impact?

How often will you progress monitor with the team?

REFLECTION

Reflection is often seen as the last step in the inquiry process, but you need to look at this as ongoing. What we mean by that is twofold when it comes to reflection: While it should be a part of every step in the process, inquiry by its nature also means that although on the placemat it seems like the last step, there is really no last step in inquiry because we should always keep learning and growing at the same time we celebrate reaching each milestone that we focus on when it comes to our priorities.

Reconsider the following questions from Figure 3.1:

1. What did you learn while engaging in this cycle?
2. How did this impact students in a positive way?
3. What improvements did you make to your practice?
4. What did you stop doing so you could have more room to focus on what matters?
5. What would you do differently next time?

CONCLUSION

We hope that drafting your priorities helped you see how the collective inquiry process can strengthen the joint work that teams engage in. This book offers several invitations to jot down notes and get insights through the Leading With Intention sections and stories, but it's the work and how you come together that will give you the greatest opportunity to learn about yourself as a leader and learn from your colleagues. You may need to reread this chapter because we are not just asking you to be more intentional; we are asking you to be almost methodical in how you approach your most important priorities. Too often, leaders do not engage in this deep work and end up with initiative fatigue and burnt-out staff who don't believe their voices are valued.

The next chapter focuses on professional learning networks. When it comes to professional learning, the content that your team and colleagues choose is important, but so is how they come together to learn. The two of us have spent a lot of time and effort creating spaces where adults feel valued and heard. That has led to a much deeper learning experience and an increased commitment to the work.

Whether we are talking about instructional leadership team meetings, instructional coaching, PLCs, faculty meetings, or district-facilitated professional learning, the environment we set—and the connectedness we feel as a group—matters greatly to how deep we go with our learning. This leads to our next chapter on creating professional learning networks.

REFLECTION QUESTIONS

- What are the four steps in the collective inquiry process?
- How does Judith Warren Little's (1990) research help us understand the nuances of collaboration and what we need?
- What are four types of evidence that Bernhardt (2018) asks us to use in school improvement?

HOW DID WE DO?

By the end of this chapter, you will have learned to

- Engage in the four steps of the collective inquiry process
- Make connections between self-awareness, human interconnectedness, and the priorities leaders establish for their schools or districts
- Define four types of evidence that will help evaluate impact as well as establish areas of focus

Collective Inquiry KWLH Chart

Take some time to consider what you have learned after reading the chapter, and then think about how you learned it.

K	W	L	H
WHAT DO I KNOW?	WHAT DO I *WANT* TO LEARN?	WHAT HAVE I LEARNED?	HOW DID I LEARN IT?

Call to Action

Consider one of the strategies that we offered within the chapter (e.g., Five Whys, Realm of Concern, Collective Inquiry Cycle Placemat), and try it in the next week. Before you engage in the activity, consider the following questions.

- What do you want it to look like?

- What are you hoping to learn by engaging in it?

CHAPTER 4

Creating a Learning Network to Focus This Work

By the end of this chapter, you will

- Recognize the difference between professional learning and professional development

- Identify the important aspects of effective professional learning and development

- Describe how professional learning and development are related to effective networks

- Consider specific ways to foster an atmosphere in your meetings or professional learning sessions that engages learners academically, socially, and emotionally

- Reflect on how to engage in a reciprocal transfer of learning that helps you grow in your own leadership self-awareness

Take some time to reflect on the topic of professional learning and development. Ask yourself what you *know* and what you *want to learn*, and write your responses in the KW columns of the following KWLH chart. As you begin reading the chapter, consider what you have learned that is new for you, and although it might be difficult, consider how you learned it.

- What is your experience with professional learning and development? What was your best experience? What was an experience that proved less than impactful?

PROFESSIONAL LEARNING KWLH CHART

K	W	L	H
WHAT DO I KNOW?	WHAT DO I *WANT* TO LEARN?	WHAT HAVE I LEARNED?	*HOW* DID I LEARN IT?

By the end of this chapter, I want to...

-
-

Creating human interconnectedness and meeting around a common purpose can be very profound. These encounters can happen with something as simple as the Meetup app introduced in Chapter 2. Many years ago, Peter's nephew Ali moved to California. Not knowing many people in the area, Ali joined Meetup because a young woman, Janie, was organizing hikes on the Central Coast. Ali thought it would be a great way to get healthy and meet people at the same time. A few years later, Ali married Janie, and they now have two kids together.

When Peter's sister Trish passed a couple of years ago, his brother-in-law, Hassan (Ali's dad), was going through a profound loss. Ali encouraged him to join Meetup because he thought it would get Hassan out of the house and provided a different way to experience his grief. Hassan began doing a Meetup hike every week. It didn't make the loss of his wife easier, but it did help him find some joy in life again.

The two of us (Mike and Peter) believe that how we come together to connect, learn, and create actionable steps around our priorities should be a Meetup every single time. Those moments when we have the opportunity to meet up with our colleagues should be life-giving experiences where we engage in a reciprocal transfer of learning.

In this chapter, we explore self-awareness, efficacy, human interconnectedness, and how all three are central to how we learn together as a school community while trying to achieve our main priorities. We cannot achieve those priorities set out in the collective inquiry process without our school community.

PROFESSIONAL LEARNING NETWORK MINDSET

Imagine participating in a professional learning network (PLN), within your building, district, state, or region, that helps foster what we have outlined so far in the book. Imagine that as leaders you look at your faculty or district instructional leadership team as a PLN, not merely just colleagues you work with every day. That learning network, whether within your school or district or with colleagues from across the state, helps you develop self-awareness as a leader. It nurtures not just relationships but also this human interconnectedness that engages you academically, socially, and emotionally. We strongly believe as leaders that you can foster this anywhere you like.

In *Call to Action: Bringing the Profession Back In*, Michael Fullan and Andy Hargreaves (2016) state that

> professional learning is often like student learning—something that is deliberately structured and increasingly accepted because it can (to some) more obviously be linked to measurable outcomes. (p. 3)

The authors go on to define professional development:

> Professional development involves many aspects of learning but may also involve developing mindfulness, team building and team development, intellectual stimulation for its own sake, [and] reading good literature that prompts reflection on the human condition. (p. 3)

The easy part of professional learning and development is to define it. The hard part is to get it right. Too often, educators are subjected to a "sit and get" where they are fed content at workshops, conferences, faculty meetings, or school leadership meetings, which can feel like taking a drink from a firehose. These sessions are often isolated from each other, as opposed to deeply connected experiences that foster growth.

Anxiety diminishes efficacy, and excitement increases efficacy (Bandura, 1997, 2010), so if teachers and leaders don't feel connected when coming together for professional learning and development, it can lead to anxiety that diminishes positive learning. It's not just a feeling of discomfort, which can sometimes lead to deeper learning; it's actually more a feeling of confusion because you don't even know why you're in the room in the first place. In our experience as coaches, we have had teachers confide in us that they don't know why they are at leadership team meetings or district-run professional development sessions, because clarity was never provided for why they should attend. The two of us have asked participants why they are present at a workshop or conference, and answers ranged from "I don't know" to "The district is making us do it." Sadly, this creates a missed opportunity for intentional and deep learning. And even more tragic is that teachers and leaders rarely see their faculty meetings and leadership meetings as a venue for professional learning.

This chapter will focus on what effective professional learning could look like in your school, district, region, or state, but equally important is how you set up an experience for participants so they understand the focus of the learning before they step foot in the room, what you can all do during the session, and how you can keep it ongoing so that the learning you and your staff engage in doesn't seem so disjointed.

WHAT THE RESEARCH SAYS EDUCATORS NEED

If you imagined the best professional learning experience you could have, what would it look like? Perhaps you have already experienced it and can answer the question right away. Or perhaps you have yet to experience professional learning that is impactful.

Deidre Le Fevre et al. (2019) and her co-authors outline six necessary elements of effective professional learning and development:

1. **Adopting an evaluative inquiry stance:** Engaging in a problem of practice and using collective inquiry to help solve the problem

2. **Being metacognitive:** Understanding why we individually think the way we do about how and what we learn

3. **Valuing and using deep conceptual knowledge:** Understanding how the individual pieces fit together to form a greater whole that we can use in our classrooms or schools

4. **Being agentic:** Developing a sense of agency in ourselves and others

5. **Being aware of cultural positioning:** Understanding the culture of our school and district

6. **Bringing a systemic focus:** Helping all of those engaged in learning to understand the whole system and not just their individual classroom, grade level, or department

If people do not understand why they are in the room in the first place and lack an understanding of the system as a whole, the professional learning they experience may be surface level at best. Matthew A. Kraft and colleagues (2018) found that across a combined 60 studies that employed causal research designs, instructional coaches had an effect size of 0.49 standard deviations when it came to helping teachers try new instructional strategies in the classroom, but when they looked at how those strategies impacted student learning, they found an average effect size of 0.18 standard deviations on student achievement. This happens because you can learn a strategy at a workshop or a conference, but that doesnt necessarily mean that it will be used correctly or that you will take the time to understand how it impacts student learning.

The two of us would like to get back to more research on professional learning, but we feel it is important to lay out what professional learning and development should look like. After all, we discussed self-awareness and self-efficacy in Chapter 1, fostering human interconnectedness in Chapter 2, and collective inquiry in Chapter 3, and now it's time to help you visualize what all of this can look like and how it connects to more intentional leadership.

We're going to begin with a story from Peter about an experience he and Mike had over the past two years with the Instructional Leadership Network (ILN), which was the brainchild of Mike in his work as the assistant director of professional learning for the Washington Association of School Administrators (WASA). The ILN was Mike's response to the needed work on operations and management during the pandemic to a more intentional refocus on teaching and learning.

Knowledge Through Storytelling

How to Create a Learning Network

A group of over 100 directors of teaching and learning from across Washington state sat in a conference room in Des Moines, Washington, in October 2021. It was the first time many of them had been to a conference since before the COVID-19 pandemic, and they were eager to learn more about what this two-year-long hybrid learning network would look like. The directors had signed on to the professional learning journey, and many of them spoke that morning about the fact that not only did they need to learn from researchers and their colleagues, but they also had the deep need to feel connected to other leaders from around their region and across their state.

After everyone came in to say good morning to each other, grab some breakfast, and find a seat, our project coordinator for the Washington Association of School Administrators (WASA) stood at the microphone to welcome everyone to what we titled the Instructional Leadership Network (ILN). WASA's leadership team and I had spent a few months designing success criteria for the two-year professional learning program. The ILN was Mike's brainchild, with two lead advisors and one outside evaluator (retired superintendent) completing the team. The ILN had funding from the state's Office of Superintendent of Public Instruction (OSPI) and support from WASA executive director Joel Aune.

On that first morning when we all sat together, as the project coordinator stood at the microphone, he welcomed everyone and began reading *The Circles All Around Us* by Brad Montague (2021). In Chapter 2, you read that I was not on board with kicking off a two-year program with the reading of a picture book. It's odd, because I was an elementary school teacher and principal and I loved reading picture books. It's just that I didn't think it was a good idea at a workshop. I learned quickly that I was wrong. Picture books were a perfect kickoff. The coordinator read, "In the circles all around us, everywhere that we all go, there's a difference we can make and a love we can all show." If you'd like to hear the story read aloud, search for *The Circles All Around Us* on YouTube and look for Storytime with Suzanne (2022).

According to Penguin Random House (2021),

This is the story of a circle. When we're first born, our circle is very small, but as we grow and build relationships, our circle keeps getting bigger and bigger to include family, friends, neighbors, community, and beyond.

Mike was very intentional in choosing this book. He wanted people in the room to understand that, if the ILN did this journey correctly, everyone in the room would end the journey as a member of a much larger circle. Considering this was happening during a time when COVID-19 was prevalent, the *Circles* book provided the audience with some much-needed comfort.

Over the next two years, the team of five, along with close to 200 directors of teaching and learning, met monthly in a hybrid approach through the ILN. There were three in-person events each year and monthly three-hour sessions that focused on instructional leadership, collective efficacy, and other timely topics.

The ILN used the online engagement tool Mentimeter to engage participants and formally assess their learning, and Mentimeter helped us understand the needs of the group so we could plan for the next session. We had a "Lunch and Learn" for one hour each month based on what we had learned from the audience and used learning protocols during each session to engage the audience but also to model strategies they could use for teachers and leaders in their districts. The feedback from participants each time and overall, after the two-year professional learning journey completed, was very positive.

WHAT FOSTERS EFFECTIVE PROFESSIONAL LEARNING?

Anyone working in school leadership understands the importance of developing a PLN that is impactful. It is needed now more than ever before. Burnout among leaders is high, and educators are leaving the profession. As leaders and teachers, we all need to feel connected to our colleagues and to the reasons we got into education in the first place.

According to the National Association of Secondary School Principals (2020), 42% of principals surveyed indicated they were considering leaving their position. Among the most common reasons they cite are the following:

- Working conditions
- Compensation and financial obligations
- High-stakes accountability systems and evaluation practices

- Lack of decision-making authority
- Inadequate access to professional learning opportunities

One of the results that can emerge from effective professional learning, such as we described earlier, is the role of the reciprocal transfer of learning. Reciprocal transfer not only involves the transfer of learning from the person in the role of teacher or facilitator but also includes learning that transfers back to the person in the role of teacher or facilitator through the following methods:

- Discussions around data and evidence
- Team discussions when planning for learning
- Developing success criteria with members of a team or the audience engaged in learning
- Engaging in conversations about specific content with learners
- Engaging in collegial conversations about the work with colleagues inside and outside their work environment

Every time our core leadership team met, we looked at the overall success criteria and made sure we tied specific success criteria to it for the monthly learning sessions and Lunch and Learns. What we learned, and continue to learn, is that leaders are looking for opportunities to connect with others and learn from those networks, too. The experience we created over the last two years was life-changing for all of us. In fact, it created lifelong friendships and some of the most powerful learning we have ever engaged in.

Here we'd like to map the example of the positive professional learning experience side by side with Le Fevre et al.'s (2019) six elements:

- **Adopting an evaluative inquiry stance:** All participants were asked to consider an adaptive challenge or a problem they were facing in their district. We engaged in collective inquiry with the audience.
- **Being metacognitive:** In year two, we placed a heavy emphasis on metacognition and used strategies such as KWLH charts to help participants engage in the metacognitive process.
- **Valuing and using deep conceptual knowledge:** Given that we had monthly sessions, we could focus on conceptual knowledge, which we had to do because so many of the

participants came from different backgrounds and contexts.

- **Being agentic:** We developed a sense of agency in ourselves and others through learning strategies and using those strategies back in our schools and districts. We engaged in deep conversations during professional learning sessions where leaders and teachers felt heard and seen.

- **Being aware of cultural positioning:** We strove to deepen our understanding of the culture of our school and district. For this we used demographic data to understand the experience level of our teachers and leaders, as well as perceptions data such as surveys and empathy interviews.

- **Bringing a systemic focus:** Our goal was to help all of those engaged in learning to understand the whole system and not just their individual classroom, grade level, or department.

When considering the following Leading With Intention questions, consider what you learned from our story. The process we used can be applied at the state, building, or district level.

LEADING WITH INTENTION

- How often do you consider the experience of the participants and not just the learning for the professional learning sessions?

- What tool do you use for formative assessment when it comes to the needs of participants in professional learning and development?

- How do you allow time for participants to get to know each other? How well do you know your staff?

In order to provide impactful professional learning, you must build in time for self-reflection to help participants gain self-awareness. However, you also need to build in time to create an experience that focuses on deep human interconnectedness, which we described in Chapter 2. This is not just about workshops and conferences, but about how you approach any learning you engage in at the building and district level.

# WHAT'S YOUR STORY?

How do you build in time for people to connect with one another, whether at a faculty meeting or a professional development session? How does Le Fevre et al.'s (2019) guidance fit into the professional learning you are referring to? Write your thoughts here.

It's not just the content that is important, but the experience you offer to others. Again, anxiety diminishes efficacy, and excitement increases it. As leaders, you must have an unreasonable hunger and drive to create those experiences that will increase efficacy because, for far too long, "sit and get" sessions have only diminished the efficacy of educators. In the following story, Mike explains why we should all be more unreasonable.

Knowledge Through Storytelling

How Being "Unreasonable" Led to a More Impactful Professional Learning Experience

---

Without exception, no matter what you do, you can make a difference in someone's life. You must be able to name for yourself why your work matters. And if you're a leader, you need to encourage everyone on your team to do the same.

(From Unreasonable Hospitality by Will Guidara, 2022, p. 99)

My Italian grandmother died seven years before I was born, but her lessons of hospitality have been ingrained in me for over 60 years. My grandmother always had a pot of sauce on the stove bubbling away. Similar to the sourdough bread starter that spread across the world during the pandemic, she never started her sauce from the beginning. She purposefully and intentionally added to its base every day; whether it was a few tomatoes, some chopped garlic, a sprig of basil, a parmesan rind, or a chicken neck, she knew just what needed to be added to the sauce to improve on what she had. The sauce was there for a reason. Its smells would draw a family member, friend, or neighbor into her home where she would welcome them with a seat at the family table.

On an Oprah Winfrey show several decades ago, Oprah discussed how the art of welcoming a person into your home does not begin when the person enters the front door. The welcome should begin as soon as the guest enters your property. "According to Oprah, a home should feel like a 'warm hug'" (Oprah Daily, 2022).

As the assistant executive director of WASA, I had the responsibility of creating learning experiences for leaders across the state of Washington, and I was one of a team of six kicking off a new two-year monthly hybrid professional learning journey for school building leaders across the state of Washington called Next Level Leaders. These memories of my grandmother and Oprah's advice made me stop and think about what they meant for me in my role. I had also recently read *Unreasonable Hospitality* by Will Guidara (2022). All three of these influences led me to ask our team how we could think differently about how we might start the opening session of Next Level Leaders.

(Continued)

(Continued)

Pre-learning Letter

Our pre-learning letter to registrants not only shared our excitement for the program and our success criteria; it also included a brief survey as a way to get to know each learner on an individual basis. The survey included the typical questions asking why participants signed up and what they hoped to learn during the two years. The difference was that I also asked participants to include their favorite nonalcoholic beverage, favorite snack, and favorite quote. To our surprise, they took these questions seriously. Even though they did not know why we asked them, participants were very specific in letting us know their answers!

The Welcome *Before* Entering the Learning Space

With my grandmother, Oprah, and *Unreasonable Hospitality* as guides, our planning team embarked on a plan to create a warm hug of hospitality for participants before they entered our learning space. We created not the usual single registration and welcome table, but five. Registrants were greeted and welcomed at the first station with their name tag. From there they were directed to the second table where they received a customized glass with a Next Level Leader logo on the front and a quote from *Unreasonable Hospitality* on the back. This had them making comments like "This is a different kind of welcome" or "Wow, I have never received a glass like this before I walked into a workshop."

At the third station, however, their body language and comments shifted. This was where they received their favorite beverage. Our team went to many stores to find their very specific choices! Some participants shook their heads in disbelief. Some became emotional while others just laughed uncontrollably. The pace slowed as they walked to the fourth station where each participant received their customized Next Level Leaders journal.

The fifth and final station was a magical one. In more instances than not, well-known educational leaders, who present around the world, stay behind the scenes until they are introduced to come on stage. We wanted this experience for participants to be different. Both of our facilitators of learning individually greeted each person, handing them a "pen to capture learning" as they entered our learning space. Participants felt overwhelmed by the individual attention and motivated to engage.

Adding to the Sauce in a Purposeful Manner

Once in the room, we wanted to engage in a conversation about the importance of what the participants experienced just before they entered the learning space. To facilitate this learning, our team read the picture book *Beneath* by Cori Doerrfeld (2023). In this book, a grandfather takes his grandson on a walk, and as they walk, the grandfather shares with the boy that it is not just what you see that matters; it is also important to explore what lies *beneath*. Using this book as a leadership metaphor, participants began to understand and engage in *beneath* conversations with each other about two things:

1. How the welcome made them feel as participants and learners and how it changed their mindset about being in the program

2. How doing a similar welcome with the teams they lead could have an impact on the ultimate work of supporting student learning

This conversation was facilitated using a protocol Mike created, shown in Figure 4.1, called the Rainbow Connection using three quotes pulled from *Unreasonable Hospitality* (Guidara, 2022) and *The Art of Gathering* (Parker, 2018).

Participants reflected individually, discussed in triads, and then moved to a group of six to come up with a word or phrase about the welcome. Each group of six captured their word or phrase on a large piece of chart paper, which was purposefully displayed in the room as a constant reminder throughout the workshop of the feeling of what was *beneath* the welcome they experienced.

A Full-Circle Closure Only Enhances a Powerful Welcome

In professional learning sessions in which our planning team has participated, the closure is often disconnected from the welcome. More often than not, we have left workshops wondering how the closure connected to the learning. Speakers want to draw out the emotion during this moment as a way of finishing strong without fully making a learning connection. During the closure of the opening of the session, we again drew upon how we started the learning portion of the workshop.

We read the book *Beneath* (Doerrfeld, 2023) again, but instead of our team reading it, several participants read the pages. Subtly and yet symbolically, we were turning the learning points of the welcome and the book over to them to lead with their teams. Finally, we had them silently read the words and quotes from the Rainbow Connection protocol still hanging around the room. As they were reading the words on the wall, we unveiled on the screen a large word cloud collectively representing the words from each team's chart.

As in all word clouds, the words most frequently used were highlighted in size and boldness. It was easy for participants to see how the design of our learning entrance was an intentional welcome hug before they entered the learning space and how, throughout our time together, we added just the right learning ingredients. Finally, our goal was to model *Unreasonable Hospitality* (Guidara, 2022) in an educational setting. Soon, teams would return for another school year. We are hoping this learning experience transformed their practice with their teams.

(Continued)

(Continued)

FIGURE 4.1 ● Rainbow Connection Protocol

Rainbow Connection Protocol

Form a RED, ORANGE, and YELLOW triad or a GREEN, BLUE, and PURPLE triad.

Discuss each quote and be ready to share its essence with another triad.

Rainbow Connection Protocol

Supplies

- Red, Orange, Yellow: Three quotes from *Unreasonable Hospitality* (one in each color)
- Green, Blue, Purple: Three quotes from *The Art of Gathering* (one in each color)
- Large chart paper (one for each rainbow group)
- Markers for chart paper

Process

- Hand one quote to each participant.
- Ask participants to individually reflect (while you quietly play "Rainbow Connection").
- Invite participants to find a triad (Red, Orange, Yellow group or Green, Blue, Purple group). Each triad will discuss their three quotes with the purpose of being ready to share the essence of the three quotes with another triad. ("Rainbow Connection" plays during the transition.)
- Have each Red, Orange, Yellow triad find a Green, Blue, Purple triad. Each rainbow group of six will discuss their quotes.
- Using a large piece of chart paper, ask each rainbow group to write down a word or phrase (no more than six words) of synthesis. ("Rainbow Connection" plays during the transition to a group of six.)
- Gather in a whole-group rainbow arc (using the entire room). Each rainbow group will chorally share out their word or phrase.
- Hang chart paper around the room as a learning anchor for the length of the workshop.
- Review chart paper around the room at various points during the workshop.

Created by Mike Nelson@SuitguyMike

Source: Guidara (2022); Parker (2018); Williams and Ascher (1979).

You might be reading this story thinking you could never do all of that. Perhaps, what you need is not to do it all, but to do some elements. The following Leading With Intention activity is meant to help you reflect on that.

LEADING WITH INTENTION

Mike provided examples of how we welcomed participants into the Next Level Leaders kickoff such as handing out badges with names and cities but no titles and giving people their favorite drink.

- What part of that welcome could you commit to?

- In what ways do you welcome participants into the professional learning you design?

- How do you surround yourself with creative people who can design a welcome where people feel valued and seen?

DEVELOP INTERCONNECTEDNESS

Planning for the event took a great deal of self-awareness because we wanted to present the content of the professional learning kickoff in a way that we had never been greeted with when entering a learning experience. We set out to foster human interconnectedness from the very moment participants walked into the conference.

Peter's original intake form focused on the name, position, and educational priorities of the incoming participants, but Mike asked to add different questions focusing on favorite drink, snack, and educational quotation. Due to Mike's inspiration, Peter asked two more questions on the intake form, which proved to be invaluable and helped the individuals filling out the form to practice a bit of self-awareness themselves.

One question was "What would you like the Next Level Leaders team to know about you?" One participant mentioned that she was hearing impaired and would like closed captioning where possible and printed materials as well. While she thought the team would most likely do this for her in future sessions, due to the intake form the team was able to do it in the very first meeting of the Next Level Leaders program even though she had only filled out the form the day before.

The other question Peter added asked participants to upload a picture of themselves so that the team could recognize people when they entered the conference on the first day. The pictures were a sort of yearbook for all the participants and helped the Next Level Leaders team engage a bit deeper with everyone. For an example of the intake form, see Figure 4.2.

Let's take a moment here to reflect on this idea of unreasonable leadership as it relates to professional learning. The following Leading With Intention activity will help you decide your level of self-awareness when it comes to professional learning and development, and whether you just develop relationships among participants or develop human interconnectedness.

FIGURE 4.2 ● Sample Intake Form

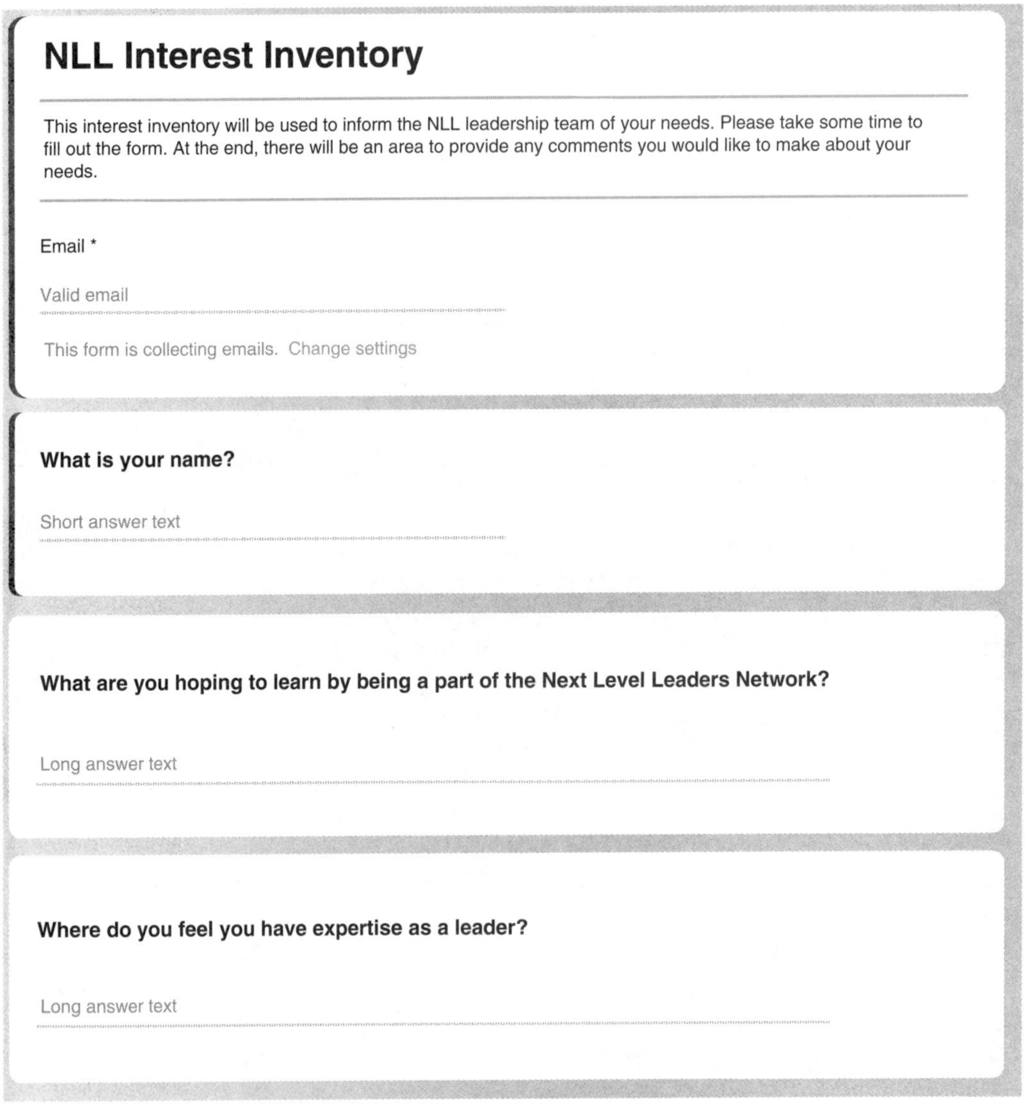

NLL Interest Inventory

This interest inventory will be used to inform the NLL leadership team of your needs. Please take some time to fill out the form. At the end, there will be an area to provide any comments you would like to make about your needs.

Email *

Valid email

This form is collecting emails. Change settings

What is your name?

Short answer text

What are you hoping to learn by being a part of the Next Level Leaders Network?

Long answer text

Where do you feel you have expertise as a leader?

Long answer text

Figure 4.2 (Continued)

Have you identified a challenge of practice? If so, what is it?

Long answer text

What are the top three priorities in your academic plan (strategic plan, building plan, district plan, etc.)?

Long answer text

What steps have you taken to enhance your personal leadership?

Long answer text

What would you like the NLL team to know about you?

Long answer text

What do you expect from the NLL program?

Long answer text

In your own words, What do you believe are the characteristics of a Next Level Leader?

Long answer text

What is your favorite type of candy bar or healthy snack?

Long answer text

(Continued)

Figure 4.2 (Continued)

What is your favorite type of candy bar or healthy snack?

Long answer text

What is your favorite drink?

Long answer text

What is your favorite educational quote?

Long answer text

Please upload a picture of yourself. Think of it as choosing a pic for the yearbook.

⬆ Add file ⬛ View folder

LEADING WITH INTENTION

In the weeks or months prior to a professional learning session within your district or school, do you do any of the following?

- Send a welcome letter with success criteria for the learning and ask participants to consider their own

- Create an intake form for participants, asking them not just basic questions like name and position, but something personal as well (Could you ask about their favorite snacks or drinks, for example, and present that small gift for them when they arrive?)

- As a team, stand outside the room welcoming people into the learning like we ask teachers to do every day with their students

- Set the atmosphere by reading a book or doing an activity that brings people together (as opposed to just jumping into the learning)

WHAT'S YOUR STORY?

Now it's your turn. Write out your unreasonable story. Where did you engage in acts that fostered awareness and connections that other people thought to be unreasonable?

CONNECTING THE DOTS OF PROFESSIONAL LEARNING AND DEVELOPMENT

We offered two stories centered on providing participants with a safe space to engage in deep and intentional learning. Now we will focus on professional learning and development, which begins with understanding the priorities of the participants. Everyone comes to professional learning with a variety of previous experiences and needs. The key is to make sure that you and your team deliver the content that the participants need, at the same time they are keenly aware of what they as the participants need.

The following is an example of success criteria that can be sent out to participants prior to a professional learning session using our collective inquiry and instructional leadership focus.

By the end of this session, participants will be able to

- Engage in a collective inquiry process that will result in choosing up to three priorities for your school or district
- Define two actions you can take to engage in instructional leadership
- Engage in actions that will help you develop self-awareness in your own leadership
- Contribute to human interconnectedness to help strengthen your level of instructional leadership
- Use metacognitive activities to help you understand your current state of strengths and areas for continued growth
- Define and foster the conditions for leadership efficacy, collective leader efficacy, and collective teacher efficacy in your district
- Engage in specific actions that create intentional implementation and result in a transfer of learning

After defining his success criteria, Peter uses Mentimeter to ask participants to define their success criteria. Most times, participants ask for strategies, but many others will provide their specific needs that usually focus on finding a balance between management and instructional leadership.

Once success criteria are established, we usually ask, "What are your top three priorities as a leader?" You may remember from Chapter 3 that we asked you to list one, two, or three priorities as a school or district. The next step is to understand why you chose those one, two, or three priorities in the first place. This includes being self-aware about our actions (see Chapter 1) and thinking intentionally about the role of transfer of learning from our needs to the impact of our actions.

CREATING A LEARNING NETWORK

Professional learning and development, whether at a leadership team meeting, a faculty meeting, or a more formal learning experience like a workshop or conference, should result in a transfer of learning. Julie Stern et al. (2021) suggest that "transfer of learning is at once incredibly simple and incredibly complex. At its most fundamental level, it simply means applying our past learning to a new situation" (p. 5). Any meeting we engage in should tie our prior learning to our present circumstances.

We would like to extend the concept of transfer of learning to the concept of a reciprocal transfer of learning. We define the reciprocal transfer of learning as what your colleagues learn from you *and* what you learn from them. We must have the mindset that when we enter a meeting, workshop, or conference as the facilitator, we are also there to learn. Such a learning mindset helps foster a learning network.

In "Essential Features of Effective Networks in Education," Santiago Rincón-Gallardo and Michael Fullan (2016) highlight eight areas that are essential when creating a network:

1. Focusing on ambitious student learning outcomes linked to effective pedagogy
2. Developing strong relationships of trust and internal accountability
3. Continuously improving practice and systems through cycles of collective inquiry
4. Using deliberate leadership and skilled facilitation within flat power structures
5. Frequently interacting and learning inward
6. Constantly connecting outward to learn from others
7. Forming new partnerships among students, teachers, families, and communities
8. Securing adequate resources to sustain the work

In the following Leading With Intention section, reflect on your one, two, or three priorities and tie them to the work of Rincón-Gallardo and Fullan (2016). How can you use the eight essential features to deepen the work?

LEADING WITH INTENTION

What are your one, two, or three priorities? Do they connect to focusing on ambitious student outcomes, developing strong relationships, or one of the other essential features? Which features do your priorities connect to?

How does the professional learning and development you provide tie to the essential features? Do you use skilled facilitation to flatten structures? Do you use protocols to help educators learn inward and learn from one another?

CONCLUSION

Being a more intentional leader means you not only develop self-awareness but also engage in actions that will help build a human interconnectedness where people feel valued, seen, and heard. We used research from Le Fevre et al. (2019) and Rincón-Gallardo and Fullan (2016) to anchor our stories in research. Are you creating stories that are anchored in research?

Too often, leaders and teachers show up to meetings where they are talked at and not talked with. You have probably experienced this once or twice in your career. How can you possibly feel inspired to try the new strategies in your classrooms or schools that you learn in professional learning and development if you have had little opportunity to develop a sense of agency?

This chapter reflected on the idea of unreasonable leadership inspired by Will Guidara's (2022) book *Unreasonable Hospitality*. We value unreasonable hospitality because at this point in time, regardless of where you are in the world, teachers and leaders are leaving the profession. The more you can find ways to be unreasonable and connect with your colleagues—and see them as partners in what you do—the more they will feel connected and want to stay with you.

To do this work, you learned from Le Fevre et al. (2019) that there are six aspects to professional learning and development, and fostering a sense of agency in others is one of these important aspects. You also learned about the eight essential elements of creating a professional learning network, and ideas about how to ensure that academic learning and social-emotional learning are at the heart of your PLN.

REFLECTION QUESTIONS

- What is professional learning and development?

- What are the six important aspects of professional learning and development?

- How did our two stories about the Instructional Leadership Network and Next Level Leaders make you feel? Did you take away a new concept?

- What are the eight essential elements of creating a professional learning network?

- How did this chapter help you think more intentionally about your one, two, or three main priorities?

HOW DID WE DO?

By the end of this chapter, you will have learned to

- Recognize the difference between professional learning and professional development

- Identify the important aspects of effective professional learning and professional development

- Describe how professional learning and professional development are related to effective networks

- Consider specific ways to foster an atmosphere in your meetings or professional learning sessions that engage learners academically, socially, and emotionally

- Reflect on how to engage in a reciprocal transfer of learning that helps you grow in your own leadership self-awareness

Professional Learning KWLH Chart

Take some time to consider what you have learned in this chapter, and then think about how you learned it. We know that can be a difficult question to consider, so we would like you to consider whether something we wrote aligns with actions you have taken. Did you take time away from reading the chapter and find yourself right in the middle of one of the situations we wrote about?

(Continued)

(Continued)

K	W	L	H
WHAT DO I KNOW?	WHAT DO I *WANT TO LEARN?*	WHAT HAVE I LEARNED?	*HOW* DID I LEARN IT?

Call to Action

Consider one of the strategies that we offered within the chapter (e.g., Rainbow Connection, intake form), and try it in the next week. Before you engage in the activity, consider the following questions.

- What do you want it to look like?

- What are you hoping to learn by engaging in it?

CHAPTER 5

Creating Your Own Learning Environment

By the end of this chapter, you will

- Take time to process the steps you take to create effective learning opportunities

- Engage with our reflection activities focused on professional learning and development and create your own experience that fosters self-awareness, a sense of efficacy, and human interconnectedness

- Consider the important role of metacognition in professional learning and development and engage with protocols to help you model metacognition for others

In this book, we have discussed self-awareness, self-efficacy, and human interconnectedness and tied them to (up to) three priorities, collective inquiry, and the ability to meet up with colleagues to engage in a reciprocal transfer of learning. What we want more than anything is for you to not just facilitate professional learning but engage with it as if you are creating your own Meetup. We want you to do more than just get together; we want you to enjoy the experience and create memories. Let's begin with what you *know*, and what you *want to learn*, when it comes to setting the environment for professional learning and development.

CREATING YOUR OWN LEARNING ENVIRONMENT KWLH CHART

K	W	L	H
WHAT DO I KNOW?	WHAT DO I *WANT TO LEARN?*	WHAT HAVE I LEARNED?	*HOW DID I LEARN IT?*

By the end of this chapter, I want to...

-
-

Use the knowledge of what you know and what you want to learn as you read through the steps for creating and engaging in professional learning and development. Keep in mind that these steps can be followed regardless of whether you are engaging with your faculty, school leadership team, or districtwide professional learning and development. We believe that the focus of the learning, which needs to be established first, should be centered on your one, two, or three priorities. One reason that tools like Meetup have been so successful is that people have done a great deal of work establishing a focus for why they meet up, and they clearly articulate that in every communication. Do you do that when it comes to your priorities?

Too often, professional learning and development seem to be done in a silo, and people who attend do not always understand why. Articulating and communicating the priorities of the school or district will go a long way to building coherence when it comes to priorities and impacting student learning. We are providing you with this chapter as a place to plan. Think of this chapter as one part summary of our book and one part appendix. We want you to think of your reflections here as a series of actions you can take right now.

STEP 1: THREE PRIORITIES

Keep in mind these two questions:

- How does what we do impact student learning in positive ways?

- How do we evaluate our own impact?

The one, two, or three priorities that were created using evidence (e.g., demographic, perceptions, student learning, and school processes data) and the input of staff and the larger school community and then refined by your school leadership team should be the focal point for the professional learning and development sessions you create for teachers and leaders.

Write your three priorities. If you only have one or two, that works for us as well. We just don't want you to have more than three priorities!

STEP 2: DEFINE YOUR SUCCESS CRITERIA FOR THE LEARNING CONTENT

Our consistent focus on intentionality brings us to Step 2. When the two of us are asked to be lead advisors in creating instructional leadership networks, we often find that the people we work with want to jump to the conversation about what speakers they should invite to the network. That is flawed thinking. Although we understand that well-known speakers can bring in participants, we also must acknowledge that we need to first define the success criteria, and then converse about which speakers fit the bill.

Success criteria, as we learned in Chapter 3, are vital to the success of the learning in any learning session. Those facilitating the learning need to look at their priorities, as well as the success criteria they created for those priorities, and define what the participants need to learn by the end of the session or the network experience. Imagine you are about to facilitate learning around the first of your priorities, each of which could be a series of professional learning and development sessions. In the following section, define one or two success criteria focused on your first priority. This will give you the opportunity to take the success criteria you wrote in Chapter 3 and go deeper and be more intentional. For example, one of our examples of a priority was "Increase the literacy proficiency rates of students." Possible success criteria could include the following:

By the end of this learning session, participants will be able to

- Define what proficiency means when it comes to literacy
- Use student learning data, such as progress monitoring, to determine the proficiency rate of students
- Define two high-impact literacy strategies that will have a positive impact on students

Now it's your turn. Use this space to write down a few success criteria for your first priority.

STEP 3: WELCOME LETTER

In our experience as facilitators and lead advisors, not everyone knows why they are in the room, and others do not feel confident when it comes to the focus of the learning. To address this head-on, we send out a welcome letter to all participants a week before our learning session. The following is an example of a welcome letter Peter sent out to participants before an assistant principal workshop focusing on instructional leadership.

Hi, Everyone,

I am looking forward to kicking off the Assistant Principal Leadership Academy for Region 10! What I'm hoping is that we can engage in a discussion on the topic of instructional leadership, which some might consider a narrow focus. I disagree, and we will discuss reasons why when we are together.

I have some content but would enjoy collaborating with you to develop the conversation together. With that being said, I have included success criteria for the session.

By the end of this session, you will be able to

- Define the necessary components of instructional leadership
- List ways we can optimally manage our time and find balance between the roles of instructional leadership and management
- Leverage collaboration through instructional practices to maximize the effectiveness of our leadership practices
- Analyze our level of student engagement in relation to what the research says
- Define some effective instructional strategies
- List ways to foster collective efficacy
- Define what evidence we collect to understand our impact

I am hoping that you will consider your needs as a leader and develop one piece of success criteria that you can share with me when we meet. I will be using Mentimeter to allow you to do that.

I look forward to seeing you.

Peter DeWitt, EdD

Peter also sent out letters asking participants to read an article prior to the learning session. This is often referred to as the flipped learning method because participants read the article to gain some understanding of the focus of the professional learning and development, and then they dialog about the article using a protocol before diving deeper into the topic during the session.

The following is an example of the letter Peter sends out for such sessions.

Hi, Everyone,

I am looking forward to working with all of you on September 6. As you know, our focus will be on fostering collective leader efficacy among school teams.

I have included success criteria for the workshop.

By the end of this presentation, you will be able to

- Define and analyze your team's ability to develop collective leader efficacy (CLE)
- Analyze which drivers are necessary for your school leadership team
- Consider how your school leaders can use a cycle of inquiry to develop a theory of action
- Build coherence between your school leadership team meetings and what the team practices in schools day-to-day
- Consider next steps in your process as a leader

I am hoping that you will consider your needs as a leader and develop one piece of success criteria that you can share with me when we meet. I will be using Mentimeter to allow you to do that. To help assist you in your thinking, we are attaching an article I wrote on the topic for the Australian Council for Educational Leaders.

I look forward to seeing you.

Peter DeWitt, EdD

These letters are meant to actively engage participants so that they are not sitting passively at the beginning of the conference being told what they will be learning. When Peter sends out the letter, he likes to include a link to the intake form. Each letter has three main points:

1. Welcome and acknowledge participants (the first step to fostering human interconnectedness and self-efficacy)

2. Define the success criteria for the workshop or webinar (this helps foster self-efficacy)

3. Ask participants to consider their own success criteria so they are prepared to share it at the session (this fosters voice and agency, which is central to self-efficacy and human interconnectedness)

Write your steps or a sample letter as if you were welcoming participants to your professional learning and development session.

STEP 4: INTAKE FORM

In Chapter 4, we introduced you to the intake form we created for the Next Level Leaders program in the state of Washington. We often use intake forms to understand the needs of participants. Intake forms are easy to create, and when we ask the right questions, they can make any professional learning session a much deeper experience. Figure 5.1 is our example of an intake form.

FIGURE 5.1 ● Collaborative Inquiry Intake Form

Collaborative Inquiry Intake Form

This form is for leaders and their leadership teams to provide insight into their main priorities based on their academic plan, strategic plan, or building level plan. There will be a follow-up form after the inquiry cycle is completed for leaders and their teams to reflect on their progress.

Inquiry

Source: Inquiry Image by Nick Youngson CC BY–SA 3.0 DEED
https://creativecommons.org/licenses/by-sa/3.0/

What is your name?

Short answer text

(Continued)

Figure 5.1 (Continued)

What is your role?

1. Teacher

2. School Psychologist/Counselor

3. Assistant Principal

4. Principal

5. Instructional/Academic Coach

6. Assistant Superintendent

7. Superintendent

8. Other

What is the name of your school?

Short answer text

:::

Will you be working with me as an individual or team?

◯ Individual

◯ Team

◯ Both

What are your one, two, three main priorities based on your academic plan or strategic plan (please number each priority)?

Long answer text

What are your intended outcomes (this would be quantitative data; e.g., "By the end of the year, X% of students/teachers..."

Long answer text

Figure 5.1 (Continued)

What is your success criteria for each priority (This can be qualitative, i.e., we will be successful when teachers engage in...)?

Long answer text

What is your *working* theory of action (if-then)?

Long answer text

What are your learning needs? Take time to speak with your team or a thought partner to decide what you would need from Peter to help you be more successful.

Long answer text

What is your favorite educational quote?

Long answer text

What is your favorite candy or healthy snack?

Long answer text

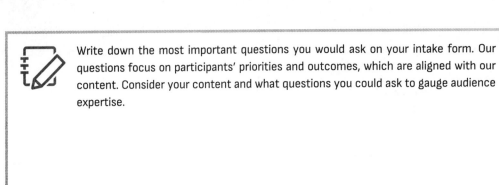
Write down the most important questions you would ask on your intake form. Our questions focus on participants' priorities and outcomes, which are aligned with our content. Consider your content and what questions you could ask to gauge audience expertise.

STEP 5: WELCOMING PARTICIPANTS

In Chapter 4, Mike shared that his Italian grandmother's way of welcoming guests and family into her home was the aroma of her red sauce simmering on the stove. Her goal was for people to join her at her family dinner table. The two of us then shared how we welcomed participants by purchasing their favorite beverage and presenting it to them at one of the welcome tables. Both examples represent establishing a culture for human interconnectedness as outlined in Chapter 2. The second example of welcoming sets the conditions for learning in a professional learning environment.

The following are some key steps for us when welcoming participants:

- We focus on the participants' names and districts, not on their positions.

- We work hard to offer participants' favorite drinks and snacks as a way to let them know we care.

- We stand at the entrance to welcome people in, just like any great teacher stands at their doorway to welcome in their students.

- A planning document is placed at each table, accompanying the success criteria participants received in their welcome letter.

- Often we begin the session by reading a children's picture book with a deep message aligned to their session (who doesn't love a great picture book?!).

Write down the steps you believe are needed to properly welcome participants.

STEP 6: CO-CONSTRUCTING SUCCESS CRITERIA

Success criteria help clarify for the audience what they will learn in the workshop. Although it's important to share the success criteria we desire for participants, after a time, we felt that something was missing. So we decided to include the audience in building success criteria with us. First we share our success criteria, and then we use an online tool like Mentimeter to ask the audience to provide their success criteria. We ask them to identify how will they know they are successful when it comes to learning at the end of the session. See Figure 5.2 for an example of participant-generated success criteria.

Tools like Mentimeter are anonymous, so there is not a downside for members of the audience to share their success criteria if they fear being recognized. After participants include their success criteria, we try our best to tie our content to what they wrote. For example, someone wrote, "Learn something that I can implement immediately." We often ask them if they co-construct success criteria with their teachers or leaders, and the answer is usually "No." We suggest that co-constructing success criteria is something they can do immediately. It's always important for facilitators of any learning to revisit success criteria because it keeps us clear and focused.

FIGURE 5.2 ● Participant-Generated Success Criteria

- Help impact our principals to impact our teachers and when we all work together we impact ALL STUDENTS.
- I always say if I learn something I can apply is a successful meeting.
- Learn something that I can implement immediately.

- Defining an outcome now to assess whether we met it at the end.
- To be able to understand success criteria, the learning goal must first be understood.
- I would like to spend time learning how to articulate with staff so that all see the need.

- Clear vision/direction of how to implement success criteria, etc with leadership team, teachers, etc.
- Clarity of the vision for the work this year.
- Make connections with our work so we can immediately put into practice.

- Learning how to achieve success.
- How to document success of my priority.
- Having a better understanding about how to document evidence of impact-various ways to evaluate succeed.

- Know how this directly impacts the work that needs to be rolled out to teachers.
- Relevant and being able to take back to our campuses to implement.
- Teamwork approach! ALL in for the kids.

- Implementing and tie into goal setting to our current CIP.... put it into practice.
- Learning practical and real life strategies to assist me in developing an effective success criteria that positively impacts ALL students.
- I would want to cultivate the expertise of all people in my organization to meet our success criteria! #bethechange.

- A common understanding on how to build positive relationships between district and campus leadership to address key issues and identify meaningful resolutions.
- Time to reflect and regroup on what our instructional pathway is and how we are doing in achieving those goals.
- A better understanding of the Evidence of impact and ways to measure progress to ensure that I am going to reach my goals.

- leadership action steps that are student-focused.
- Being able to crystallize my thinking around and be able to answer the success criteria prompts succinctly.
- To be able to develop a success criteria that meets the goal and to be able to successfully deliver it to the campus.

- Supporting school leaders in moving through the cycle efficiently to positively impact their campus outcomes.
- Have a better understanding of the outcome.
- Cultivaye the expertise of all people in my organization to meet our success criteria! #bethechange.

Write down your thoughts on how you might co-construct success criteria with your audience.

STEP 7: READING A PICTURE BOOK

Both of us loved being building principals. We saw our purpose as creating a learning culture for students and staff as well as throughout our school community including parents, patrons, and business owners. A strategy we used as principals was to select a picture book to give to each staff member. From the book, a schoolwide learning focus was launched. We include an example here of how powerful picture books can be in creating human interconnectedness within a school community.

Mike never called the meeting that takes place before the school year begins a "retreat" because no one was retreating. We called this meeting time *an advance* as we were *advancing the work*. During the school advance his first year as principal, Mike chose to read a Curious George book. Together the school team discussed personal curiosities, and they each wrote their curiosities on a large speech bubble using the sentence stem "I'm curious about _____." They shared curiosities with each other. This was, of course, a perfect example of a strategy for building a culture of human interconnectedness with staff members as described in Chapter 2.

Staff members not only made connections to each other but found ways to support each other in learning about each other's curiosities. During the advance, Mike and his staff learned the curiosities of each other and explored strategies for keeping curiosity at the forefront of their minds when planning learning experiences for children. In staff correspondences as well as in letters to families, Mike would include snippets of research.

Using the Curious George book, teachers led the learning protocol modeled by Mike with their students on the first day of school. Speech bubbles of each student's curiosity filled the hallways of the school. Teachers began to read the stories to parents on back-to-school night and asked them their curiosities. Staff meetings throughout the year focused on curiosity as it relates to student engagement.

Many wondered why Mike would use picture books while developing professional learning with staff. It is true that reading a picture book in isolation might not be the best professional learning strategy, but done with direct and intentional purpose to the learning (success criteria), it can have a profound and lasting impact on staff members' learning.

WHAT'S YOUR STORY?

What are your one, two, or three priorities for the work that you are engaged in with the people you lead? Are there picture books that might support, enhance, and solidify the learning of participants in meeting the success criteria? Write your reflections here.

STEP 8: TIME TO PROCESS

One of the lessons both of us have learned throughout our leadership experience is the need for self-awareness and an understanding of the important role of metacognition in what we do. Metacognition is often defined as thinking about our own thinking. A leader's ability to engage in metacognition will deepen their leadership. The National Research Council (2000), in their book *How People Learn*, has this to say about metacognition:

> Metacognition refers to people's abilities to predict their performances on various tasks (e.g., how well they will be able to remember various stimuli) and to monitor their current levels of mastery and understanding. (p. 12)

They go on to write that "teaching practices congruent with a metacognitive approach to learning include those that focus on sensemaking, self-assessment, and reflection on what worked and what needs improving" (p. 12).

Regardless of whether we are teachers or leaders, our ability to understand our own learning, our ability to articulate how we learn, and our ability to engage in conversations about learning with others will only help strengthen the conversations about learning that take place in our schools. If we don't understand or care about how we learn, how can we ever be a credible voice as leaders in education? There is no downside to understanding our own thinking as leaders.

Figure 5.3 outlines the two aspects of metacognition, knowledge of cognition and regulation of cognition. In some professional learning and development sessions, participants "sit and get" and don't often have time to process information. There is an assumption that participants will go back to their school or district and take time to process the learning or will be offered time back in their school or district to do so. That is flawed thinking because participants really need time to process information in the session, regardless of whether it's an instructional leadership team meeting, a faculty or district meeting, a conference, or a workshop.

Metacognitive strategies can be beneficial when asking participants to process information. For example, if participants are learning about a new strategy to use in the classroom, a metacognitive tool such as a strategy evaluation matrix can be helpful (see Figure 5.4 for an example).

FIGURE 5.3 ● Metacognition

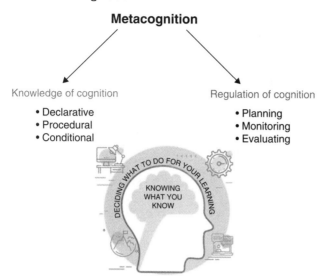

Metacognition

Knowledge of cognition
- Declarative
- Procedural
- Conditional

Regulation of cognition
- Planning
- Monitoring
- Evaluating

DECIDING WHAT TO DO FOR YOUR LEARNING

KNOWING WHAT YOU KNOW

Just because a teacher or leader uses a strategy doesn't always mean it's going to have an impact on student learning (Kraft et al., 2018). Strategy evaluation matrixes can help deepen the learning and provide an opportunity through discussion among participants to decide when the time is best to use the strategies they are learning.

FIGURE 5.4 ● Strategy Evaluation Matrix

Strategy Evaluation Matrix			
Declarative Knowledge	**Procedural Knowledge**	**Conditional Knowledge**	
Strategy	**How to Use**	**When to Use**	**Why to Use**
Learning walks	• Co-construct a walk-through protocol with teachers based on the needs of the students. • Decide on how frequently leaders and teachers would like to engage in walk-throughs. • Agree upon what follow-up to the learning walk will look like.	It's important to decide on a frequency that leaders and teachers can commit to. Perhaps they start with once a week.	Learning walks help us get a clearer picture of the learning taking place in classrooms, schools or districts. Additionally, learning walks help school communities develop a common language and common understanding around learning.

Regulation of Cognition

Planning

1. What is the nature of the task?
2. What is my goal?
3. What kind of information and strategies do I need?
4. How much time and resources will I need?

Monitoring

1. Do I have a clear understanding of what I am doing?
2. Does the task make sense?
3. Am I reaching my goals?
4. Do I need to make changes?

Evaluating

1. Have I reached my goal?
2. What worked?
3. What didn't work?
4. Would I do things differently next time?

Countless protocols are available through organizations such as the National School Reform Faculty where anyone in need of protocols can find them. Consider a strategy that you enjoy using in your leadership practices—one that you think gives you the biggest bang for your buck. Use the strategy evaluation matrix template in Figure 5.5 to help deepen your thinking around it.

When considering protocols, another important element of metacognition comes into play, which is regulation of cognition. Regulation of cognition comes down to planning, monitoring, and evaluating. For this, we are going to use a strategy referred to as Self-Regulation Questioning Stems (Tanner, 2012) and an example of the process created by our friend and colleague Jenni Donohoo (2023).

Figure 5.5 is a blank strategy evaluation matrix that we use in professional learning and development sessions to help participants process. Consider a leadership action that you use and fill out the matrix. In the space that follows, write out your reflections on how you might use this action in a professional learning and development session.

FIGURE 5.5 • Strategy Evaluation Matrix Template

STRATEGY EVALUATION MATRIX			
DECLARATIVE KNOWLEDGE	PROCEDURAL KNOWLEDGE	CONDITIONAL KNOWLEDGE	
STRATEGY	HOW TO USE	WHEN TO USE	WHY TO USE

STEP 9: HOW YOU CLOSE IS AS IMPORTANT AS HOW YOU OPEN

We often find that the desire to get people out early at the end of the professional learning day seems to take precedence over offering reflection time at the end of the workshop or webinar. If professional learning and development are seen as an opportunity to develop self-awareness and self-efficacy, as well as foster human interconnectedness among participants, then the closing is as important as the opening.

At the end of sessions, we share success criteria from the beginning of the session and ask participants to reflect on how we did. Additionally, it's important that participants are given a reflection activity to help tie the learning together. The most important aspects to a closing are these:

- A space to provide closure
- Reflection on the success criteria and to gauge how we did
- An opportunity to ask any final questions
- A call to action where people decide on their next leadership action steps

Reflect on what you think is most important for the closing of a professional learning and development session. If you work with the same participants over a period of time, you might ask them to consider what evidence they will bring to the next session that will help them understand their evidence of impact.

On the theme of how a closing is as important as a beginning, consider the greatest and most impactful professional learning and development that you experienced. What did it look like, feel like, and sound like? What part did you have in it, and how did that contribute to the success of the learning? How did it help you develop self-awareness and foster human interconnectedness? Write out your thoughts here.

Lastly, reflect on our book. What resonated for you? What are your next leadership action steps? We have added some questions to this page to help guide your thinking.

How do you focus on your own self-awareness?

How do you help foster self-awareness in others?

How do you foster human interconnectedness?

What role does professional learning and development play in your leadership?

How do you provide effective professional learning and development to those you lead?

How do you incorporate metacognition into your leadership practices?

What resonated for you as you read our book?

CONCLUSION

In this chapter, we have laid out a step-by-step guide to setting the environment of the professional learning and development we create and facilitate. From the welcome, to the content, to the metacognitive activities we employ, to the final stages when we focus on closure, we have given you the outline of what's needed to improve any professional learning experience.

We began this book with a focus on leadership self-awareness and self-efficacy. Leaders are much more successful with implementing strategies and initiatives when they understand how they lead, through internal and external self-awareness. Human interconnectedness is another important element. The stories we have presented here and those we've heard on the road are all about how people want to be a part of a community. Human interconnectedness is about personal accountability that leads to collective responsibility.

We tied this work to the priorities of your school community and then delved deeply into how to create professional learning and development experiences that help people understand why they are in the room to learn and share, as well as how to make sure the best ideas of implementation are fostered within that room.

Both of us strongly believe and have researched that professional learning and development need to change so people are not talked at but talked with so that they can share ideas and challenge each other's thinking. We hope that this book offered you not just insight into how to do that but also the opportunity to reflect on your own experiences and develop an understanding of your own legacy as a leader.

Thank you for taking this journey with us.

Mike and Peter

HOW DID WE DO?

By the end of this chapter, you will have learned to

- Take time to process the steps you take to create effective learning opportunities

(Continued)

(Continued)

- Engage with our reflection activities focused on professional learning and development and create your own experience that fosters self-awareness, a sense of efficacy, and human interconnectedness

- Consider the important role of metacognition in professional learning and development and engage with protocols to help you model metacognition for others

Please complete the L and H columns of this chapter's KWLH chart.

Professional Learning and Development KWLH Chart

K	W	L	H
WHAT DO I KNOW?	WHAT DO I WANT TO LEARN?	WHAT HAVE I LEARNED?	HOW DID I LEARN IT?

Afterword

By Shelley Harwayne, author of
Above and Beyond the Writing Workshop
(Stenhouse, 2021)

During my tenure as a Manhattan school superintendent, I took part in several professional rituals. These included weekly district office staff meetings, monthly principal get-togethers at district schools, and annual and more formal school walk-throughs at each of the 40 schools in our large urban district. Perhaps, the most powerful and memorable ritual was one created and required by our school's chancellor, the person at the helm of all 45 school superintendents in New York City. Every week, we were asked to write a letter to the chancellor. I don't recall any guidelines, but I do know that I took this assignment seriously. I relished the opportunity to have an appointment to write about my work. I valued this weekly task as a means of sharing accomplishments, queries, and challenges ahead. An unexpected benefit resulted when the chancellor jotted notes in the margins, helping me to clarify my role as a leader, think new thoughts, and try out new ideas.

It's been 20 years since my retirement, but I still have that bulging folder filled with copies of those weekly reports. Reading Peter M. DeWitt and Michael Nelson's book, *Leading With Intention*, inspired me to take out that folder and reread what amounts to the story of my life as a school superintendent.

I have come to realize that the book you hold in your hands can actually serve as a thoughtful school's chancellor, peeking over your shoulder, prodding you to clarify your role as a leader, think new thoughts, and try out new ideas. Throughout their book, Peter and Mike have asked you to pause, to reflect, to write, to tell stories, to question, to connect, to listen, and to make your work add up. In each and every chapter, they have privileged metacognition, self-awareness, and human interconnectedness, and demonstrated why those qualities matter.

Now your task is to make sure that all their thoughtful suggestions make a difference in your role as a leader, lifting the quality of your professional setting for principals, teachers, school board members, students, and their families. Many years ago, the late Vartan Gregorian, when president of Brown University, asked members of a parent gathering to stand if they were educators. He then began a round of applause for those standing, announcing, "The greatest compliment a school can receive is when educators choose to send their children to us." That rings as true for elementary, middle, and high schools as it does for universities. When we offer the highest quality of education to our students, teachers will want their own children to attend our schools. Throughout my years as an administrator, Gregorian's comment inspired me to reach for the stars. Likewise, *Leading With Intention* inspires readers to reach for the stars, to attain the highest standards imaginable in our instructional settings.

I have only one humble suggestion for guaranteeing that what you have learned from studying this book will have a positive effect on the professional setting you call your home away from home. Find a caring colleague with whom you can reread the chapters, swap jottings, provide feedback, commiserate, celebrate, visit one another's settings, and be there for the warm hug, the pat on the back, and the sincere smile whenever those comforting gestures are needed. In other words, in addition to belonging to larger professional learning networks as suggested by the authors, why not create a more intimate one? Trust in the power of two caring leaders becoming book buddies.

If I were still a principal or a school superintendent, I would reach out to another colleague who has read this insightful book, and I'd ask that we meet regularly to share our reflections, stories, and implementation plans. I can easily imagine discussing several questions:

- How can we become superintendent teachers, educating our school board members in important ways? How do we maintain our role as principal teachers when each year seems to bring more and more demands that keep us out of classrooms?

- How can we make our school professional development sessions as interactive as the chapters in this book, avoiding the image of filling empty vessels, but trusting faculty members to interact with new ideas, innovating and inspiring one another?

- How can Guy Winch's (2015) "7 Habits of Genuine People" help us when we interview potential candidates for employment? What questions could we ask that would help us know if a prospective employee is not threatened by failure, has solid self-esteem, or is not judgmental?

In addition to getting together to share responses to such questions, I would hope that we would also set dates to visit one another's schools, looking for evidence of the big ideas in this book. These might include the following:

- Visiting to look for evidence of the things we say we value in teaching and learning

- Visiting to discover moments of human interconnectedness, with students, families, and colleagues

- Visiting to appreciate genuine collaborative inquiry in classrooms as well as staffrooms

Throughout their book, the authors ask us to think about the legacy of leadership we want to leave behind. I recall returning to the Manhattan New School, after giving up my role as principal, to become the superintendent of the same school district. Touring the school, a young student looked at me and commented, "You used to be important, didn't you?" She was right. I used to be important in that school building. Principals are important people in school buildings, but equally important are the teachers, the support staff, the students, and their families, as well as the superintendent who leads from afar. The legacy of leadership that matters most to me has little to do with being called important. Rather, I want to be remembered as an instructional leader who enabled children and their teachers to do their best work. Isn't that the goal for all who led with intention?

References

Bandura, A. (1997). *Self-efficacy: The exercise of control*. Freeman.

Bandura, A. (2010). Cultivate self-efficacy for personal and organizational effectiveness. In E. A. Locke (Ed.), *Handbook for principles of organizational behavior* (pp. 9–35). Oxford University Press.

Bernhardt, V. (2018). *Data analysis for continuous school improvement*. An Eye On Education Book. Routledge.

Casey, L. (2014). *Questions, curiosity and the inquiry cycle*. E-Learning and Digital Media.

Clarke, S. (2021). *Unlocking learning intentions and success criteria: Shifting from product to process across disciplines*. Corwin.

Clear, J. (2018). *Atomic habits: An easy and proven way to build good habits and break bad ones*. Avery.

de Saint-Exupéry, A. (1939). *Wind, sand, and stars* (L. Galantière, Trans.). Reynal and Hitchcock.

Doerrfeld, C. (2023). *Beneath*. Little, Brown Books for Young Readers.

Donohoo, J. (2013). *Collective inquiry for educators: A facilitator's guide to school improvement*. Corwin.

Donohoo, J. (2023, March 2). *Presentation for the Washington Association of School Administrators (WASA)*.

Drucker, P. F. (2005, January). Best of HBR 1999: Managing oneself. *Harvard Business Review*. https://halftimeinstitute.org/wp-content/uploads/2022/03/Managing-Oneself-Peter-Drucker-HBR-1999.pdf

Eriksen, M. (2009). Authentic leadership, practical reflexivity, self-awareness, and self-authorship. *Journal of Management Education, 33*(6), 747–771. https://doi.org/10.1177/1052562909339307

Fullan, M., & Hargreaves, A. (2016). *Call to action: Bringing the profession back in*. Learning Forward.

Gates, B. (with Myhrvold, N., & Rinearson, P.). (1995). *The road ahead*. Viking Penguin.

Grinder, M. (with Yenik, M.). (2007). *How not to get shot! Taken from The elusive obvious: The science of non-verbal communication* (pp. 16, 51). Michael Grinder & Associates.

Guidara, W. (2022). *Unreasonable hospitality: The remarkable power of giving people more than they expect*. Optimism Press.

Harbinger, J. (2018, May 23). *Stop trying to be "vulnerable." Do this instead*. The Jordan Harbinger Show. https://www.jordanharbinger.com/stop-trying-to-be-vulnerable-do-this-instead/

Kouzes, J., & Posner, B. (2023). *The leadership challenge: How to make extraordinary things happen in organizations* (7th ed.). Wiley.

Kraft, M. A., Blazar, D., & Hogan, D. (2018). The effect of teacher coaching on instruction and achievement: A meta-analysis of the causal evidence. *Review of Educational Research, 88*(4), 547–588.

Le Fevre, D., Timperley, H., Twyford, K., & Ell, F. (2019). *Leading powerful professional learning: Responding to complexity with adaptive expertise*. Corwin.

Little, J. W. (1990). The persistence of privacy: Autonomy and initiative in teachers' professional relations. *Teachers College Record, 91*(4), 509–536. https://doi.org/10.1177/016146819009100403

Merriam-Webster. (n.d.). Knowledge. In *Merriam-Webster.com dictionary*. https://www.merriam-webster.com/dictionary/knowledge

Montague, B. (2021). *The circles all around us*. Dial Books.

National Association of Secondary School Principals. (2020, May 14). *With nearly half of principals considering leaving, research urges attention to working conditions, compensation, and supports*. https://www.nassp.org/news/with-nearly-half-of-principals-considering-leaving-resear ch-urges-attention-to-working-conditio ns-compensation-and-supports/

National Research Council. (2000). *How people learn: Brain, mind, experience, and school* (Expanded ed.). National Academy Press.

Nelson, M. (2023, June 20). *How superintendents can engage board members to benefit their districts.* Finding Common Ground [Blog]. Education Week. https://www.ed week.org/leadership/opinion/how-super intendents-can-engage-board-members -to-benefit-their-districts/2023/06

Odetola, T. O., Erickson, E. L., Bryan, C. E., & Walker, L. (1972). Organizational structure and student alienation. *Educational Administration Quarterly, 8*(1), 15–26.

Oprah Daily. (2022, January 30). *Oprah on the importance of having a place you feel truly at home.* https://www.oprahdai ly.com/life/a38923805/oprah-home-is- a-place-where/

Parker, P. (2018). *The art of gathering: How we meet and why it matters.* Riverhead Books.

Penguin Random House. (2021). *About The circles all around us.* https://www.penguin- randomhouse.com/books/653426/the-cir cles-all-around-us-by-brad-montague-illu strated-by-brad-and-kristi-montague/

Perry, E. (2022, September 14). *Self-awareness in leadership: How it will make you a better boss.* BetterUp. https://www.betterup.com/ blog/self-awareness-in-leadership

Rincón-Gallardo, S., & Fullan, M. (2016). Essential features of effective networks in education. *Journal of Professional Capital and Community, 1*(1), 5–22.

Ryan, J. E. (2017). *Wait, what? And life's other essential questions.* HarperOne.

Stern, J., Ferraro, K., Duncan, K., & Aleo, T. (2021). *Learning that transfers: Designing curriculum for a changing world.* Corwin.

Storytime with Suzanne. (2022, August 28). *The circles all around us by Brad Montague and illustrated by Brad and Kristi Montague* [Video]. YouTube. https://www .youtu- be.com/watch?v=evgMwLh9ugc

Sutton, A., Williams, H. M., & Allinson, C. W. (2015). A longitudinal, mixed method evaluation of self-awareness training in the workplace. *European Journal of Training and Development, 39*(7), 610–627. https:// doi.org/10.1108/EJTD-04-2015-0031

Tanner, K. (2012). Promoting student metacognition. *CBE-Life Sciences Education, 11*(2), 113–120.

Wang, F. (2021). Principals' self- and inter- personal leadership amid work intensi- fication. *Journal of School Leadership, 31*(5), 396–427. https://doi.org/10.1177/1052684 620935383

Wellington, E. (2021, May 12). *Why commu- nity and connection matter in a digital world.* PlaceLab. https://www.eqoffice.com/pla- celab/community-connection-in-digital- world

Williams, P., & Ascher, K. (Songwriters). (1979, June). Rainbow connection [Song]. On *The Muppet Movie original soundtrack recording.* Atlantic.

Winch, G. (2015, March 18). The 7 habits of truly genuine people. *Psychology Today.* https://www.psychologytoday.com/us/bl og/the-squeaky-wheel/201503/the-7-hab its-truly-genuine-people

Wooll, M. (2022, June 14). *Your workforce is lonely. It's hurting your business.* BetterUp. https://www.betterup.com/blog/connec- tion-crisis-impact-on-work

Index

A Sage Company

CORWIN HAS ONE MISSION: to enhance education through intentional professional learning.

We build long-term relationships with our authors, educators, clients, and associations who partner with us to develop and continuously improve the best evidence-based practices that establish and support lifelong learning.